BeesKnees #6:
A Beekeeping Memoir:

Volume Six: Days 501-600

The Journey of a Beginning Beekeeper

Fran Stewart

BeesKnees #6: A Beekeeping Memoir
Fran Stewart
© 2020

All rights reserved. No part of this book may be used or reproduced in any manner whatsoever without written permission from the author, except by a reviewer who may quote brief passages in a review.

Cover design by Darlene Carter

ISBN: 978-1-951368-06-7

This book was printed in the United States of America.

Published by
My Own Ship Press
PO Box 490153
Lawrenceville GA 30049

myownship@icloud.com
franstewart.com

*To those I'd choose to share my hive
(in the order in which I met you):
Diana, Eli, Veronica, and Darlene*

Books by Fran Stewart

The Biscuit McKee Mystery Series:

Orange as Marmalade
Yellow as Legal Pads
Green as a Garden Hose
Blue as Blue Jeans
Indigo as an Iris
Violet as an Amethyst
Gray as Ashes

Red as a Rooster
Black as Soot
Pink as a Peony
White as Ice

A Slaying Song Tonight

The Scot Shop Mysteries:

A Wee Murder in My Shop
A Wee Dose of Death
A Wee Homicide in the Hotel

Poetry:

Resolution

For Children:

As Orange As Marmalade/
    Tan naranja como Mermelada
(a bilingual book)

Non-Fiction:

From The Tip of My Pen: a workbook for writers
BeesKnees #1: A Beekeeping Memoir
BeesKnees #2: A Beekeeping Memoir
BeesKnees #3: A Beekeeping Memoir
BeesKnees #4: A Beekeeping Memoir
BeesKnees #5: A Beekeeping Memoir
BeesKnees #6: A Beekeeping Memoir

Introduction to Volume 6

This is it. The final hundred days.

If you've stayed with me this far, you've had a chance to enter at least a little way into the mind of Fran Stewart.

Scary, isn't it?

This is the volume where we encounter a leap year day. I always wanted to have been born on February 29th. But I wasn't, doggone it. Or as my cats and my grand-dogs would say, humangone it.

Enough of that. Enjoy the rest of this journey.

I do promise that once we've gotten through this volume, there will be more—not about bees, but about life in general. I can't publish that book though until I can think of a great title.

Any ideas?

[**2019 Note:** I have a title. Now I just need to write the book.]

>   --Fran
>   from my house beside a creek
>   on the other side of Hog Mountain GA

Fran Stewart

Day #501 Bees with Back Problems?
Saturday, February 25, 2012

I got to thinking about what happens to bees if they have back problems. They probably just die. I never heard of a bee chiropractor.

I'd like to tell you a story.

Years and years ago, in what feels like another lifetime, I was the passenger in a car that was T-boned, and the door caved in on me.

That was before I knew about chiropractors. A visit to an orthopedist resulted in nothing except that I saw some really cool X-rays of my now-crooked spine, that, when viewed from the back, went down, over, down, showing how the upper vertebrae had been nudged to the left and had stuck there. It was a miracle it hadn't severed my spinal cord. The damage to my neck and back left me in pretty bad shape, and I limped around for days, finally giving up in pain and despair and simply staying in bed. I hurt so much I wanted to die.

We had some friends who lived near Washington DC at the time. Karen found sitters for her children and drove to Vermont unannounced, breezed in and took over the management of the house. She cared for my children, cooked meals, cleaned up, babied me, and eventually got me up (sort of) and walking (kind of).

When I finally went to a chiropractor, doubled over with the pain, I walked out after the appointment upright for the first time in weeks.

So, I'm going to praise chiropractors for the rest of my life. I'm also feeling pretty grateful to Karen. She moved from DC to Florida several years after she saved me, and I'd seen her only once since then when she and her husband Dan drove through the Atlanta area.

But for the past couple of days I've been visiting them in their comfy house in Ormond Beach. I had intended to leave my phone turned off and buried in my suitcase the entire four days, but I chose not to, since my niece is still hospitalized, and I didn't want to miss any updates. The good news is that her eyes are open now, and she is able to recognize people. Keep the good thoughts flowing her way, please.

One of the byproducts of that decision to keep my phone on was that I was able to take photos.

My first goal in coming here to Florida was to catch up with Karen on a lot of what I've missed for the past few decades; the second was to walk barefooted on the beach. Now that I've done those, I'll be heading home tomorrow.

And I might even have some pictures to share with you.

BeeAttitude for Day #501: *Blessed are those who keep in touch with old friends, for they shall feel a deep sense of connection.*

Fran Stewart

 ## Day #502 Driving Home Safely Today
Sunday, February 26, 2012

I hope the 8-hour drive is uneventful. I'll be listening to the last 8 or 9 CDs of *Pillars of the Earth* as I drive. That 36-CD set was the biggest recorded book I could find in the library. Or rather, it was the biggest one I hadn't read yet.

There is something so anonymous about Interstate rest stops. There's a constant round of unnamed people using the restrooms, eating, stretching, and diving back into their cars, all of which look so similar.

EllieBug stands out like a clown at a funeral. People laugh at the yellow polka dots and point and give me a thumbs-up as I drive. I'm happy to brighten their day a bit.

Please wish me a safe trip home today.

BeeAttitude for Day #502: *Blessed are those who fly carefully, for they shall return to the hive in safety and be welcomed joyfully.*

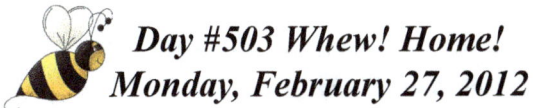 Day #503 Whew! Home!
Monday, February 27, 2012

Thank goodness for friends and family. Whenever I leave for a few days, I have to arrange cat-sitters to come in to feed and play with my girls (and scoop the litter boxes). Thank you Veronica and Millie! Of course, it's easier now that I have two cats instead of the eleven I had at one time. All of them indoor cats.

Come to think of it, when I had eleven cats, I didn't take many trips.

That's what so comforting about hobby beekeeping. Beekeepers truly are not necessary to the health of the hive. A beekeeper could go away for weeks at a time, months, years even, and the hives would keep going. They might swarm. They might re-queen themselves. But they'd most likely survive and would probably even thrive (as long as neighbors within a five-mile radius don't use pesticides and herbicides).

Rob Alexander, the beekeeper who is caring for my two hives, told me that mine were the healthiest in his bee yard, probably because I never bothered them very much. Instead of opening the hive boxes once a week or so—which is what most backyard beekeepers do—I just let them grow. Yes, I did feed them during that horrible spell of drought in August when there was NO food available for them, but other than that, I pretty much left them alone, particularly after I developed an allergy to bee stings.

Yesterday I couldn't come home to beehives on my back deck, but I did come home to two loving cats who, contrary to the myth perpetrated by dog-people, do not ignore me.

BeeAttitude for Day #503: *Blessed are those who live in harmony with the world around them, for they shall have ample honey, glorious sunshine, fresh water nearby, and bounteous pollen, which is all anybee needs.*

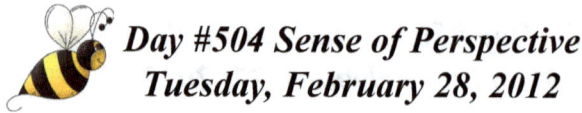 Day #504 Sense of Perspective
Tuesday, February 28, 2012

You know what the trouble is nowadays with taking a vacation? When you get back, you have several hundred emails to go through.

It feels like punishment of a sort, plowing through the junk to get to the few jewels here and there.

When bees fly back to the hive after a long foraging trip, they get welcomed back—because they're carrying nectar and pollen—and there's probably no buildup of extra chores they have to do. Of course, on the other hand, they don't really get any sort of vacation. Ever.

I had a chance to watch the sunrise over the Atlantic; I saw dolphins; I ate yummy food I wouldn't get here in Georgia (at least, not in my house, since I don't like to cook); so, I guess "200 emails" is a small price to pay for such a great time.

And Erica is doing much better, by the way. Thank you for asking.

BeeAttitude for Day #504: *Blessed are those who stay in touch with old friends, for they shall have a sense of perspective.*

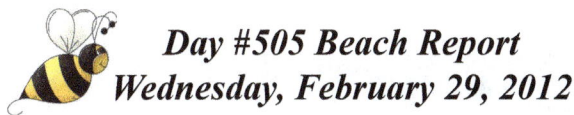

Day #505 Beach Report
Wednesday, February 29, 2012

Happy Leap Year Day. I thought you might enjoy seeing a little bit of my recent vacation.

I didn't see a single honeybee at the beach. Of course, I do wonder if bees like the Atlantic shore. The wind was pretty stiff most of the time.

I didn't see any bees in Karen and Dan's yard either.

This yellow flower bloomed on the sand dune beside the shore, just at the base of an observation platform. I spotted it after the sun came up.

Even though there were no bees, I did see a couple of little critters that I'd like to share with you. The closed shell you see here contained a live animal, and I had to give it a little kiss before I eased it back into the receding tide.

This next little guy was as perky as they come. Too bad s/he was empty. Of course, if there had been anyone home, the shell wouldn't have looked so uncannily like a face.

Looks rather like Chewbacca, doesn't it? The eyes, the hair, even the nose . . .

Then I found this announcement, from a lighthouse commission report in 1868:

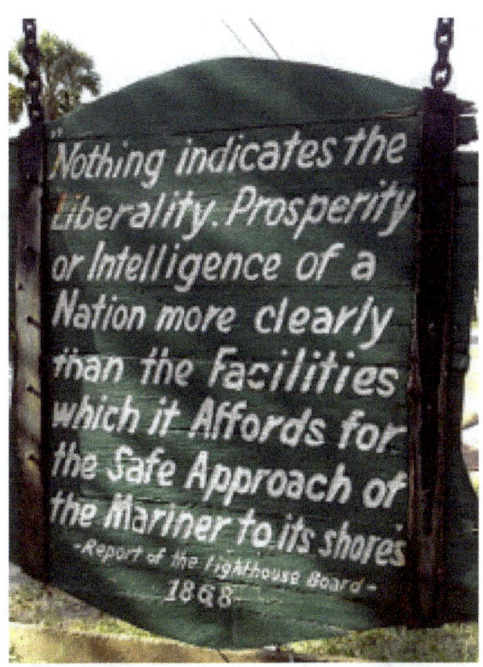

It still has a good message today.

My shins are still sore from the miles we walked along the beach at daybreak (and midday and sunset) – but it was worth it.

Thanks, Karen and Dan.

BeeAttitude for Day #505: *Blessed are those who watch where they're flying [or walking], for they shall see wonders.*

p.s. Miss Polly found a box while I was gone...

Day #506 WMES Walls
Thursday, March 1, 2012

For more than a year I've been watching the walls of the library in Woodward Mill Elementary School take shape as professional muralist Kristie Chamlee works her magic on them.

She started by simply painting the top blue. Since the walls are 14 feet tall, it was a bit of a challenge.

Then she progressed through various stages, and I watched them all develop.

You can see she's added clouds and land here:

And then trees and a barn. She had great fun drawing a red birdhouse around the fire alarm you can see in the previous picture, changing it from this:

to this:

Of course, that was all last year. This year, she's painting the remaining walls of that huge room, and it's spectacular. Just yesterday I dropped in and took this picture of the waterfall over in the back corner.

And then there's the picture of the Woodward Mill water wheel in the reading alcove.

One question: how do you fill up beanbag chairs that have gone flat?

BeeAttitude for Day #506: *Blessed are those who make the world a more beautiful place, for their names shall be sung in thanks.*

Day #507 Another iPhone Joke
Friday, March 2, 2012

Okay, I can't resist this.

Yesterday I needed to remind myself to do something, and I wasn't next to a piece of paper, so I whipped out my phone and held the button down. Siri came on and said, "What can I help you with?"

"Remind me to call my agent tomorrow morning at nine," I said.

She thought about it and came back with, "Here's your appointment; should I confirm it?"

Ordinarily I say yes, but what she'd come up with was "Call be engine."

I decided to delete this one and try again, speaking more clearly, so I told her, "No."

"That's okay," she said. "You're way too busy anyway."

I went and found a piece of paper.

BeeAttitude for Day #507: *Blessed are those who use humor when it's appropriate, for they shall delight in the laughter.*

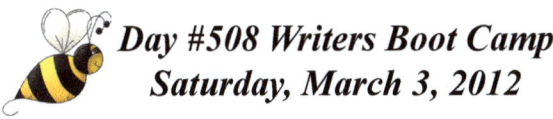 Day #508 Writers Boot Camp
Saturday, March 3, 2012

This week I've been going to Woodward Mill Elementary School to speak to the fifth-grade classes. They have a "Writer's Boot Camp" each year, and I thoroughly enjoyed speaking to each of the classes last year. This year, I'm doing the same thing again.

We're talking about verbs, and the importance of using effective ones when they revise their compositions.

One of the exercises I use allows them to fill in the blanks with either nickel words or dollar words.
    1. The lion _____ across the grassland.
    2. I _____ my grandfather's paintings.
    3. My grandmother loves to _____.
And so on. You could use **nickel verbs**:
    1. walked
    2. like
    3. smile
But think how much more interesting, exciting, compelling these sentences would be with **dollar verbs** such as:
    1. stalked
    2. abandoned
    3. sky-dive
We had quite a discussion about the story that's implied when we say I abandoned my grandfather's paintings. Don't you want to know why?

Let's see...another sentence could be
    1. Honeybees _____ (fly/buzz/sting/pollinate...)

BeeAttitude for Day #508: *Blessed are those who stretch their minds, for they shall find more room in their brains.*

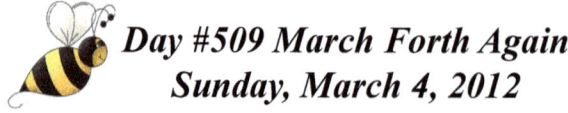

Day #509 March Forth Again
Sunday, March 4, 2012

Here it is again, the only day of the year that tells us what to do:

March Forth !

Today I plan to march forth by buying p.m.terrell's newest book, Vicki's Key. It promises to be as exciting as her previous 12 books. She's a dear friend as well as a professional colleague, and you might want to check her out at www.pmterrell.com

Then I'd better get busy writing my own next book. I still haven't decided whether the title should be Brown as Dirt or Brown as Fudge.

I'm leaning toward the fudge. Why does that not surprise me?

[**2019 Note:** That 7th Biscuit McKee Mystery turned out to deal with arson, so I named it Gray as Ashes. I love flexibility!]

BeeAttitude for Day #509: *Blessed are those who eat with joy, for their tummies shall be filled with goodness.*

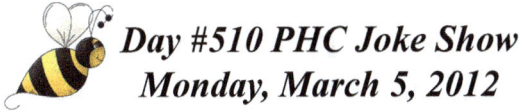 ## Day #510 PHC Joke Show
Monday, March 5, 2012

Saturday evening I listened to the Prairie Home Companion show on Public Radio. You've probably heard of Garrison Keillor, even if you've never listened to him. Once or twice a year they have a Joke Show. The entire show – the whole two hours – is chock full of the silliest jokes imaginable. The jokes are usually grouped:

- <u>knock-knock jokes</u>

Knock-knock. Who's there?
Sanctuary
Sanctuary?
Sanctuary much!

- <u>change-a-light-bulb jokes</u>

How many surrealists does it take to change a light bulb?
A penguin.

- <u>animal jokes</u>

Why was the cow crying?
Because she had a moo disorder.

- <u>chicken jokes</u>

Why did the chicken cross the Moibus strip?
To get to the same side.

And then there are the miscellaneous jokes, such as:
What do you call an existentialist breakfast cereal? Raisin d'Etre
Why didn't the oyster give up her pearl? She was shellfish.

You gotta love the folks who come up with these.

BeeAttitude for Day #510: *Blessed are those who laugh hard every day, for they shall spread joy and it will bounce back at them.*
"Hey, bees, I think you used that attitude before, or something a lot like it."
"Buzz off, Frannie. We like that one."

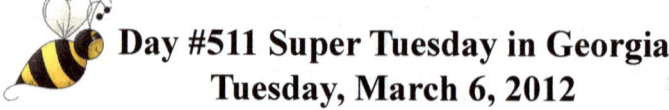 Day #511 Super Tuesday in Georgia
Tuesday, March 6, 2012

Here's my prediction for Georgia's Super Tuesday: Regardless of who wins, we're going to be swamped at my precinct. Maybe at yours, too.

Did you remember from one of my previous posts that poll workers set up the polls on Monday afternoon or evening, finish setting up Tuesday morning, power up the machines and set out all the signs before the polls open at 7:00? Once they are sworn in at 6 am, they can't leave the polling place until the very end of the evening. If we want meals, we have to bring them ourselves. I still bless the man who brought 5 large pizzas to us during the last presidential election.

Poll officials help people through the voting process all day long, deal with any questions or disputes, and take hourly counts to be sure the number of votes on the machines tally with the number of voters who have checked in.

After the polls close, they verify the voter-count, close the machines, pack up all the supplies, lock the bags that contain the critical paperwork, and clean up the precinct space.

After that the precinct manager and an assistant manager return the bags of supplies to the elections office.

They may, if they're lucky, get home by 9:30 or 10:00, but on a busy election day like this year, it could be closer to midnight.

When you vote, whatever day your state holds elections, be sure to thank your poll workers. I promise you, it will mean a lot to them.

BeeAttitude for Day #511: *Blessed are those who volunteer to help their neighborhood, their county, their state, their hive. They shall have the satisfaction of a job well done.*

Day #512 Blatant Promo - A Great Workshop
Wednesday, March 7, 2012

I'm writing this Tuesday evening after a 3:30 a.m. to 10:30 p.m. Election Day. 3:30 is when I got up; 10:30 is when I got home. So I hope you'll forgive me if I'm brief, indeed. I just want to share something fun with you—

On May 5th, I'll be conducting a writers' workshop at the Harris Arts Center in Calhoun, Georgia from 9am to 4pm.

I hope you'll consider signing up – or at least let your writing friends know about it.

BeeAttitude for Day #512: *Blessed are those who provide water for us bees, for they shall have a happier yard as a result.*

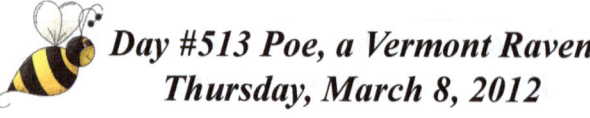
Day #513 Poe, a Vermont Raven
Thursday, March 8, 2012

Years ago my family spent our summers at a little cottage (which Vermonters call a "camp") on Lake Iroquois.

One day a raven showed up on our deck, walked around, nodded at us, and flew off. He became a regular visitor. We called him Poe.

Photo Credit: Pixabay (pexels.com)

The neighbors down the road—a lovely gravel road overhung with interlacing tree branches—called him "The Judge." Other folks along the road—he visited ALL of us—had different names for him. But he seemed to spend more time with us than with them. Maybe it was because of the cactus on our deck that he liked to peck at.

Photo Credit: Oziel Gómez (Pexels.com)

We read the numbers off the band on one of his legs, called the University of Vermont, and were referred to Dr. Bernd Heinrich, whose studies of communication in ravens were world famous (among ravenfolks, that is). He told us that he was studying the homing instincts of the ravens, wanting to know if they would keep his yard as their home territory, or if they would fly off and never return. "Just let him be," he advised.

At any rate, one day Poe showed up with his legs horribly tangled in fishing line. He could fly, but because his legs were bound together, he couldn't walk, and his hopping was impeded because his balance was off. If I've ever seen a cry for help, Poe was giving one. I called Dr. Heinrich immediately, and he said he'd be there as quickly as he could drive the back roads.

When he arrived and walked down our gravel path toward the camp, Poe began ducking his head and spreading his wings. Dr. H mimicked the action, and the two of them carried on what looked like a conversation of ducks and bows and wing (arm) flapping.

I handed Dr. H a big bath towel. He wrapped Poe in it, and I was astonished that Poe immediately settled down. "When he can't move his wings," Dr. H told us, "he just relaxes." I think it also helped that Poe knew who was holding him.

I brought out my nail scissors and, while Dr. H held Poe, I snipped the fishing line. The skin around the multiple tangles of line was horribly swollen, so each individual length of plastic wrapped around his leg had to be cut separately, working down through the layers of line.

As I worked, Dr. Heinrich explained that ravens frequently get caught in cast-off fishing line when they grab up fish that were once hooked and somehow broke the line, trailing it through the water after them as they swim. Ravens use their feet to manipulate a fish as they eat it, so when a raven catches a fish that has fishing line attached to it, the raven can easily get the line wound around first one foot, and then as it tries to disentangle itself, around the second foot as well.

It wasn't a simple operation. It took me about 20 minutes to get it all off, although it seemed like hours. I was drenched in sweat by the time I finished.

Dr. H checked Poe carefully and announced that once the swelling was gone, Poe would most likely be fine. "A few more days, though," he said, "and Poe wouldn't have made it." He took Poe home with him for recuperation.

Fast forward to 2012: Last night, my son and I drove to Georgia Tech to hear Dr. Heinrich speak about his research "From the Bees to the Birds: Animal Communication." He changed the title on us, though, and said he'd rather talk about bees and moths.

I took copious notes, and I'll be sharing some of what he said over the next few days.

And, by the way, before the lecture, my son and I had a chance to speak with Dr. H. We mentioned Poe and the fishing line, but he didn't remember it at all. What was the adventure of a lifetime for us was just all in a day's work for him.

BeeAttitude for Day #513: *Blessed are those who question "why," for they shall be surprised by some of the answers.*

[**2019 Note:** If you'd like to find out more about ravens—particularly the seven who live at the Tower of London—may I suggest you read *The Ravenmaster* by Christopher Skaife.]

Fran Stewart

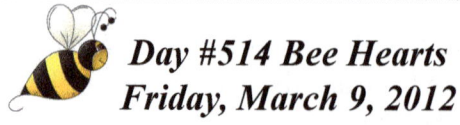

Day #514 Bee Hearts
Friday, March 9, 2012

Yesterday I told you I was going to highlight some of the information from Dr. Bernd Heinrich's lecture at Georgia Tech. Here's the first amazing (to me) bit of information that I had never heard before.

Bees and other sorts of six-legged critters such as moths and dragonflies don't have a heart in their thorax, the way we humans would expect. In fact, their heart looks more like a fat blood vessel. It runs the length of their body on the dorsal (top) side. The bee's heart pumps cool blood, which it has collected from the abdomen, up the body, down through the "waist," and into the thorax, where the contraction of the muscles there warms the blood before it goes into the head. Once it's warm, it circulates through the tissues and down the body, gradually dumping its heat. By the time the blood gets toward the bottom of the abdomen, it's as cool as the outside temperature.

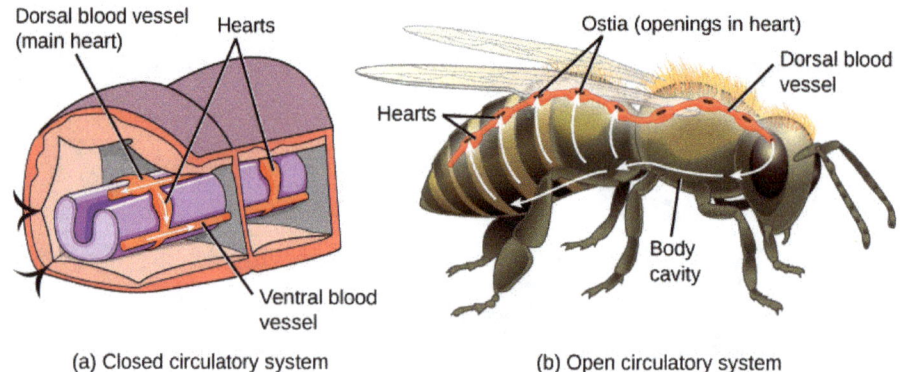

Photo Credit: TexasGateway.org

Bees never worry about warming their rear ends. It's the thorax that is the important part. If they get too hot while they're out foraging, they can dump out the contents of their honey crop (where they store the nectar and begin its transformation into honey). Seems like quite a waste to me, but then I suppose the alternative would be the death of the bee. So it's better just to lose that load of nectar.

BeesKnees #6: A Beekeeping Memoir

Tomorrow I'll tell you how bees beat their wings.

BeeAttitude for Day #514: *Blessed are those who let us BEE, for they shall hear our song every warm day.*

Day #515 How Bees and Moths Beat Their Wings
Saturday, March 10, 2012

Here's another goody I wouldn't have expected.

Dr. Heinrich explained in his lecture that the muscles bees use for wing movement don't move the wings directly. Instead, they compress and expand the thorax in micro-movements. It is those tiny expansions and contractions that push the wings up and down.

Photo Credit: Pixabay (Pexels.com)

I do wonder if hummingbird wings work the same way. Maybe by the time I've read Dr. H's books, I'll know the answer to that.

BeesKnees #6: A Beekeeping Memoir

Photo Credit: Pixabay (Pexels.com)

Tomorrow: How bumblebees hatch their eggs.

BeeAttitude for Day #515: *Blessed are those who open their windows in the spring, for they shall feel more connected to those of us who live outside always.*

Day #516 Aftermath of the Tsunami
Sunday, March 11, 2012

I know I said I'd be talking about bumblebee eggs today, but I found this beautiful message from the people of Japan in the aftermath of the force 9 earthquake and tsunami that hit one year ago on March 11. It moved me to tears. I'd like to share it with you. If you don't want to type this long string, try Googling "Japan tsunami arigato."

https://www.youtube.com/embed/SS-sWdAQsYg

This is the way the world is supposed to work.

[**2019 Note:** I just watched this video again and was as much moved as the first time around.]

I'll be back tomorrow with the bumblebees.

BeeAttitude for Day #516: *Blessed are those who go out of their way to help others, for their own lives shall brim over with love. Arigato.*

Day #517 How Bumblebees Hatch Their Eggs
Monday, March 12, 2012

I'm so used to reading about honeybees, I sometimes forget about the Bumblebees. They're a native pollinator. They were here to greet every set of people that have wandered to this land, and if we don't kill them all off with pesticides and herbicides, bumblebees will still be around to greet our twenty-times-great-grandchildren.

Photo credit: Michael Hodgins (Pexels.com)

You know, I'm sure, because I've told you how the honeybee queen lays her eggs (up to 2,500 a day) in the honeycomb, one egg in the bottom of each cell. The worker bees then care for the larvae.

Bumblebees are different. Each female bumblebee lays her eggs in a little clump and SITS on them, to warm them with the heat in the bottom of her abdomen. Remember, I told you a few days ago that the bee heart pushed the blood up into the thorax where it's warmed by muscle movement. When the warm blood leaves the thorax, it passes along the bottom of the abdomen. That's why the mommy bumblebee can warm her eggs. The heat passes from her heated blood through the layers of her body and onto/into the eggs.

Fran Stewart

Isn't that magnificent?

Tomorrow: Ravens.

In the meantime,

Happy Birthday Darlene !
Is that enough exclamation points for you?

BeeAttitude for Day #517: *Blessed are those who avoid stepping on us bees, for they shall have a brighter springtime.*

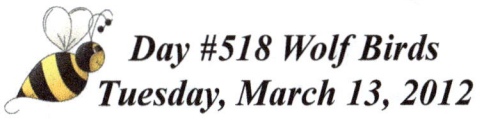

Day #518 Wolf Birds
Tuesday, March 13, 2012

Dr. Bernd Heinrich calls the raven a "wolf-bird." The reason?

I'm glad you asked.

Photo credit: Audubon.org

In the wild, ravens tend to follow wolves around the forest, knowing that the wolves will eventually make a kill, and the ravens will be ready for cleanup detail. Ravens are incapable of killing great big animals for themselves; they have to depend on another carnivore for that job. Of course, ravens are omnivores, so they don't have to rely on that part of the cycle of life in order to find food.

Dr. H said that in his research on the communication among ravens, he tried to lure them to his study area with freshly dead calf carcasses. Unfortunately, the ravens were smart enough not to approach anything he left out. But as soon as a large carnivore made a kill – ahh! Raven-feast-time!

Coming up tomorrow: How loud is a raven?

BeeAttitude for Day #518: *Blessed are those who strive to understand others, for they shall have better conversations.*

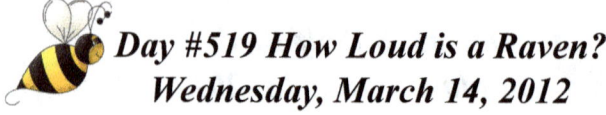

Day #519 How Loud is a Raven?
Wednesday, March 14, 2012

Would you believe Dr. Bernd Heinrich has heard ravens gathering around a wolf-killed moose carcass from a mile away?

That's all he had to say about that.

I've told you before that I have ravens that visit my yard, but Dr. H said he'd never heard of ravens in the Atlanta area. So now, I have to figure out how to get a picture of those big black birds. A birder who attended the same lecture I did spoke with me afterwards and said if I could get photos, she'd be happy to try to identify them. "And if they ARE ravens," she said, "I want to see them!"

I always thought that crows hopped and ravens walked. I even taught that to my grandchildren.

"No," Dr. H told me, "Some crows can walk."

Phooey. Guess I was wrong.

Of course, now that I think about it, why would meat-eating ravens be interested in the ground around the bottom of my bird feeder?

Unless they're after the earthworms.

They're probably crows after all.

[**2019 Note:** Nope. They're crows. Big, big birds, but definitely crows. They don't have the distinctive hairs on top of their bills or the shaggy-looking throat feathers.]

BeeAttitude for Day #519: *Blessed are those who get their facts straight, for they shall have to apologize less often.*

Day #520 The Ides of March & Bumblebees
Thursday, March 15, 2012

A couple of days ago, Petie Ogg, one of the regular commenters on this blog, asked if I had a photo of a bumblebee sitting on her eggs. I haven't been able to find one, but I'm going to keep on looking.

I've read, though, that the bumblebee queen lays only about six eggs at a time. When they hatch, they help her with caring for the next set of eggs, and so on. She gradually builds a little colony (never bigger than the size of half a grapefruit) and at the end of the season, she creates queen and drone eggs and waits for them to hatch. Then she and all her workers who've helped her over the summer die off.

The baby bumblebee queens and drones hibernate through the winter. Come Spring, they start the cycle all over again.

And, in the true spirit of the Ideas of March, here's a warning:

If you find a comatose bee
nestled in the dead leaves
during the winter,
leave it alone.
Don't assume it's dead.
It may very well be
a hibernating
bumblebee queen.

BeeAttitude for Day #520: *Blessed are those who leave us BEE (we said that already, didn't we?), for they shall encourage the next bee-generation.*

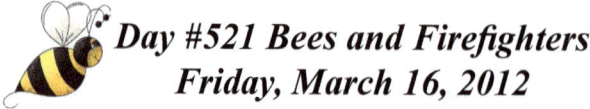 Day #521 Bees and Firefighters
Friday, March 16, 2012

Two meetings this week – and both were packed full of information. Tuesday evening was the monthly Gwinnett Beekeepers meeting, and the speaker was Dave Arnold, who's an expert in landscape management with wildlife in mind.

Here are the plants he recommended for bees (and some for butterflies, too):
- Button Bush
- Snapdragons
- Goldenrod
- Aster
- Alfalfa (let it bloom)
- Anise Hyssop
- Borage
- Mint
- Spanish Needle

I'd never heard of several of them, but I'm going to get out my books and catalogs.

How many of these are found in your yard?

Speaking of yards, Dave said that there are more than 45 million acres of lawn in the United States. Lawn – pesticide and fertilizer-ridden, a veritable desert for bees and other pollinators.

If you have that kind of desert around your house, how about considering a change to a pollinator-friendly lot?

And then, Thursday evening, the Gwinnett County Citizen Fire Academy. Whew! This is going to be a busy twelve weeks. I'll share some pictures with you when I do the ride-along, and when I try crawling through a "burning" building (fake smoke). That won't be for another few weeks, though. We have to learn a lot of skills before they put us into those yellow suits.

BeesKnees #6: A Beekeeping Memoir

Tomorrow I'll tell you about how I surprised the Fire Chief.

BeeAttitude for Day #521: *Blessed are those who do what they can to make the world a better place, for they shall benefit from a feeling of accomplishment.*

Day #522 How I Surprised the Fire Chief
Saturday, March 17, 2012

Gwinnett County Fire Chief Bill Myers greeted our Citizen Fire Academy class Thursday evening with a little talk about the Values that are important to the Fire Department.

"Our Mission," he said (and there was a handout, too), "is to Save Lives and Protect Property. Our Vision is to Deliver the Highest Quality of Service to all Customers, and the Values we hold as vital to our department are Truth, Trust, Respect, and Unity." He pointed overhead, where four flags hung from the classroom ceiling.

A blue one to our left said TRUTH, a green one said TRUST, an orange flag said RESPECT, and a red one carried the word UNITY. He gave a little speech about how those particular colors were chosen. I don't recall why blue was chosen for Truth, but Trust was on a green flag because in the deepest, coldest part of winter, we trust that spring (green) will come. Orange represented the school colors of the number 1 school in Gwinnett County, which has an excellent school system, and Unity was on a red flag, because fire trucks (the symbol that unifies the whole department) are red.

I raised my hand and said, "Did you know that you inadvertently chose chakra colors that were appropriate?"

He didn't have a clue what I was talking about.

I explained that the ancient system of explaining the energy of the body assigns red as the color of the first chakra, which represents community, foundation, UNITY. The second chakra (orange) is where creativity is centered in our bodies (and certainly where we must have RESPECT for ourselves). The green chakra is number four, the heart chakra—and it is in our hearts that we must feel TRUST; when we're openhearted, trust flows out. Finally, the fifth chakra, represented by the color blue, is the throat chakra, the place in the body from which we speak our TRUTH.

Isn't it amazing that a department with a budget of $76 million a year, which employs 845 men and women, and serves a county of over 800,000 people, from 30 strategically placed fire stations, subconsciously built its value statement on an ancient tradition for health and healing?

I think it's wonderful indeed.

BeeAttitude for Day #522: *Blessed are those who tap into ancient wisdom, for they shall bee whole.*

Fran Stewart

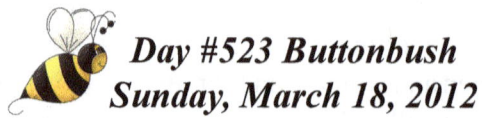

Day #523 Buttonbush
Sunday, March 18, 2012

So, I went looking for the Buttonbush I listed on Day #521 and found lots of Internet info sources about *Cephalanthus occidentalis*. All of them said that the buttonbush is highly beneficial to honeybees and bumblebees.

The University of Texas Wildflower Center website has plenty of colorful pictures of buttonbush. Here are a few - and all of them, by the way, list "unrestricted usage," so I'm not infringing on any copyrights:

The first two photos—the green one and white one—were taken by by Andy and Sally Wasowski of Burnet TX, who call themselves the Botanical Missionaries:

This next photo that shows the red fruit form is by Joseph A. Marcus of Canyon Lake TX

And finally, Sandy Smith of Sunset TX shared this clump of fruit. Note the little critter (only the legs are showing) on the leftmost fruit. Is it a spider?

The buttonbush can grow to 10 feet tall. Here's a photo taken by Carolyn Fannon.

Buttonbushes like all kinds of soil, but particularly wet ones. And they like shade. I'm going to think about planting one down by the creek.

BeeAttitude for Day #523: *Blessed are those who are curious about how life works, for they shall be endlessly entertained.*

Day #524 Am I Way Too Busy?
Monday, March 19, 2012

I would have liked to go to Eagle Eye Books in Decatur Saturday to see Cathy Kaemmerlen, who spoke about her book *The Buzz on Honeybees*. One of the regular readers of this blog emailed me about Cathy's presentation. Thank you, Mary G. I appreciated the heads-up, and was sorry I had to miss it. I hope you enjoyed it twice – once for you and once for me.

Kaemmerlen is an author, actor, and storyteller whose latest book is about – what else? – honeybees. I love the idea that someone is speaking at schools, teaching young people to respect the pollinators, sending a message with a great deal of humor and animation, so they'll remember the lesson (hopefully) all their lives.

Instead, I was singing in a Mozart concert for the Gwinnett Choral Guild. Why are there so many worthwhile things that I want to do? Why do they all seem to happen at once?

BeeAttitude for Day #524: *Blessed are those who do what they love and love what they do, for they shall feel fulfilled.*

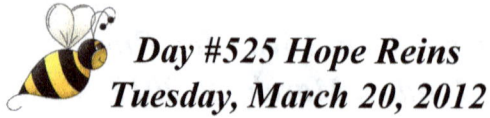

Day #525 Hope Reins
Tuesday, March 20, 2012

I know a woman who volunteers at an amazing equine therapy place in the Raleigh NC area called Hope Reins.

She feeds and cleans the horses, freshens their stalls, and does all sorts of very necessary work, simply because her heart goes out to these gentle horses, all of whom have been rescued from ghastly conditions, brought back to health, and given a chance to interact with children who need the kind of love and intuitive care that a horse can give.

After my experience with Daisy, the therapy horse who helped me overcome some of my fears, I can truly appreciate the value of such work.

I'd just like to acknowledge the folks at Hope Reins, and all the fine organizations that find a need and do their best to meet it.

BeeAttitude for Day #525: *Blessed are those who reach out to help, for they shall walk taller, stand prouder, breathe deeper.*

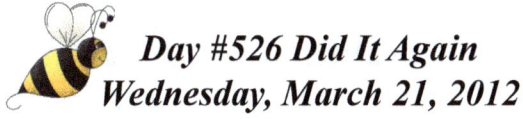

Day #526 Did It Again
Wednesday, March 21, 2012

Well, I did it again. Got my facts wrong.

Yesterday I wrote about the woman who volunteers at Hope Reins. "She freshens the stalls," I told you. Nope. I was wrong. After Kathi read the blog post yesterday, she gently corrected me.

At Hope Reins, the horses are loose in the fields. They don't live in stalls. They have shelters they can run into or out of as they wish. They're free to roam, free to play, free to enjoy their life. And, at the same time, they delight in being able to help the children who come there for the kind of love a horse can give. They are trained to help those children, and through the training process they frequently "train" their trainers. Train them to understand why some horses, and some people, respond with anger when they are simply hurting.

BeeAttitude for Day #526: *Blessed are those who are open to insights about bees and horses and people, for they shall be richer than they can imagine.*

Day #527 The Declaration of Arbroath
Thursday, March 22, 2012

I'm constantly surprised by what I dig up when I'm researching my books. The other day, I discovered the Declaration of Arbroath, which was written (in Latin) and signed on April 6, 1320. It was drawn up at the Abbey of Arbroath, which is how it got its name.

The declaration itself is very long, and rather wordy, but here's a small portion that struck me as admirably pertinent:

It is, in truth, not for glory, nor riches, nor honors that we are fighting, but for freedom – for that alone, which no honest man gives up but with life itself.

The Scots were asking the Pope to support their bid for political independence. We're talking almost 700 years ago, yet the words sound eerily modern, don't they?

It really doesn't matter what you're interested in, you can always find something more to learn about it. All you have to do is look.

What will you investigate today?

BeeAttitude for Day #527: *Blessed are those who like to explore—lands, bee-yards, ideas—for they shall find delightful surprises.*

Day #528 Citizen Fire Academy - Class #2
Friday, March 23, 2012

Thursday evening I attended an incredibly exciting Citizen Fire Academy Class. The dozen class members sat through the classroom portion of the session, learning first about medical operations/EMT training (how the ambulance crews work). In the Gwinnett County Fire Department, all firefighters receive extensive EMT training, far more than what is required by the federal and state governments.

[**2019 Note**: Since I wrote this, the GCFD has upped their requirements. Now every single would-be firefighter goes through Paramedic training, which is much more extensive than the requirements for EMTs. Why? Because most of the calls to 911 are for medical reasons, not fires.]

Then we were taught "Incident Command" (who's in charge at a fire and why). Any one supervisor is in charge of no more than 5 to 7 people. That supervisor reports to the next one in the chain of command, who is responsible for no more than 5 to 7 supervisors. And so on up the line to the Fire Chief, to whom four departments report.

We learned how jobs are assigned at a fire. Divisions indicate a geographical area.
- Numbered Divisions are assigned vertically **inside** a building. For example, in an apartment fire, if your crew is assigned to Division 1, then your job would be to go into the first floor and do whatever needed to be done there, while Division 6 would take the sixth floor, and so on.
- Lettered Divisions are on the **outside** and they progress clockwise around the house. If you get to a fire and you're assigned to Division A you know you'll be responsible for the front of the house, while Division B will move to your left and cover that (left) side; C covers the back, and Division D is the right-hand side.

Groups, on the other hand, are assigned functions. If you're assigned to the Ventilation Group, for instance, then your job is to set the fans to blow the smoke out of the whole building (after the fire is out, of course). Likewise, a commander could assign you to Ventilation Group, Division 2, and you'll know precisely what you're supposed to do (ventilate) and where you're supposed to do it (second floor).

After the classroom portion of the class, District Commander Chief Wayne Mooney led us all out into the station bay, where his vehicle sat. He opened the back and slid out an enormous tray that held more equipment than my kitchen contains. He walked us through the process he uses at a major fire and showed us how he pulls magnets from the lid of one of the handy little boxes on the back of the tray and places them in the appropriate rectangles marked on the sturdy built-in white-board chart, so he can see at a glance who is where at any given time.

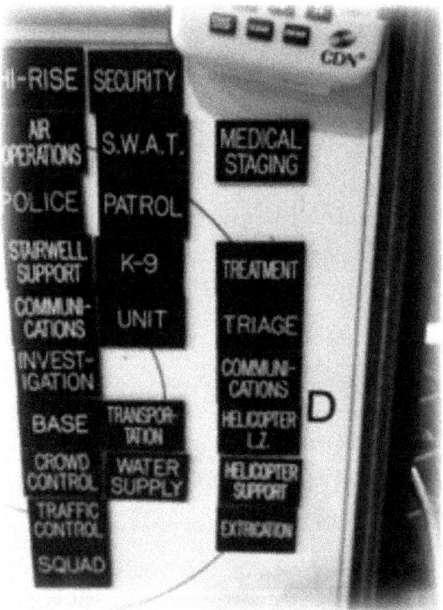

He has a different magnet for every unit (engine, ladder truck, car, ambulance...) that might be there, and every situation that might be going on (triage, helicopter, investigation...).

White magnets indicate cars (CAR 1, CAR 2, CAR 3 and so on), red ones were for the fire trucks (ENGINE 1, ENGINE 23, LADDER 5 . . .)

Other colors showed other types of situations, items, and functions. And he even had a marker in case he ran out of magnets.

The white board was divided into blocks where he could put magnets to show
1. where it was
2. who was there
3. what they were doing

As he explained all this, the ambulance and ladder truck, which had both been out on a call, returned. We all had to step aside so they could pull in through the doors at the back of the station and past us up to the front so they'd be ready to take off at a moment's notice.

Lt. Thomas then jumped into the back of the ambulance and began to show us the equipment.

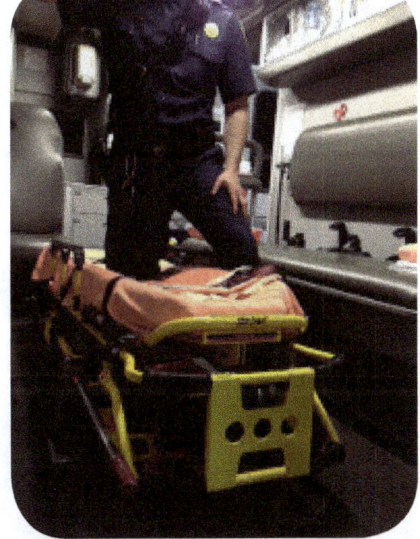

I was perched on the step at the back of the vehicle when an alarm sounded. We were shooed out of the way, firefighters jumped into the ladder truck and ambulance, and they were gone. Just like that.

There couldn't have been more than fifteen seconds between the sounding of the alarm and this picture of the ambulance lights on and the truck beginning to move.

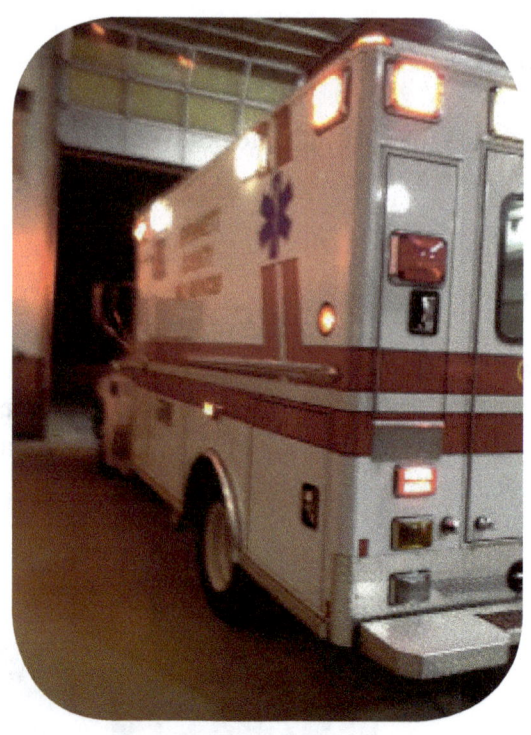

You may notice in the next picture that the ambulance driver brakes and waits for the fire truck to pull out in front. At a fire, the truck is more immediately necessary (usually) than the ambulance. The medic part of it comes later.

We class members were all shooting pictures like crazy through the whole process. I wish I could share them all with you, but I don't want to jam your computer. I would like to leave you with the two photos below, though. After the ladder truck was out of sight, I noticed four pairs of shoes on the floor of the bay, where the four men assigned to the ladder truck had jumped out of them and into their gear.

Let's hear it for the firefighters.

BeeAttitude for Day #528: *Blessed are those who put out clean water for the birds and who put a stick or a rock in there so we bees can drink safely.*

Fran Stewart

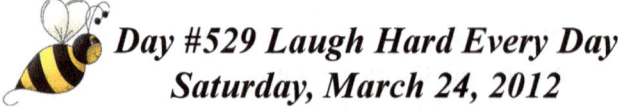 Day #529 Laugh Hard Every Day
Saturday, March 24, 2012

One of my intentions this year is to Laugh Hard Every Day

Last night I watched a compilation of Carol Burnett Show sketches and laughed till I thought I was going to fall off my chair.

What was it about the curtain rod through the Scarlett costume that is so timelessly funny? Or the horse doing number 1 AND number 2 on the set (completely unplanned!) as Carol tried to sing?

I wonder if bees have any sense of humor in their lives? Do they chuckle over a particularly strange arrangement of asters, for instance? Do they get a kick out of a more than usually enthusiastic waggle dance? Do they actively look for laughing brooks or twinkling reflections?

No. I guess not.

That's too bad. We could all gain a lot from laughing hard every single day.

BeeAttitude for Day #529: *Blessed are those who laugh at themselves, for they shall never grow bored.*

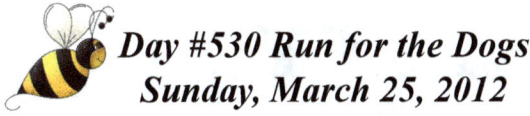

Day #530 Run for the Dogs
Sunday, March 25, 2012

Yesterday I left my house at 5:45 a.m. to drive to my friend Karen Krotz's house. She and her husband and I piled into their fully loaded car and went to the Suwanee Town Park to set up Karen's booth for the Run for the Dogs event.

Karen also happens to be my massage therapist. She'd brought along a folding tent-top to cover her booth area, a folding massage chair and all the necessary supplies to go along with that (like disposable face-cradle covers), a "sign-up-for-my-newsletter" list, clipboards, a donations bucket, a candy dish, folding table, tablecloth, business cards, pens, and most likely a dozen other things I've forgotten to list. Thank goodness they had a big trunk on their car.

I had agreed to help her by talking to people, showing them the sign-up sheet ["and you could win a free one-hour massage"], handing out her business cards, letting people know where her office was located [less than a mile from here], and asking if people wanted a 5-minute chair massage.

In return for my help, she'd told me to bring a sample set of my books and bookmarks to hand out to folks.

We were all set up and ready to go in record time.

The event was designed to raise money for dog rescue groups, and featured a 5K run. Before that was a two-times-around-the-park Fun Run, which Karen and I (and her wonderful dog Lady) translated into a Fun Walk. Practically every person there had a dog. I was delighted at how well behaved they all were (people and dogs alike <<<>>>). At the beginning Karen and I got green t-shirts, and Lady got a red bandanna. At the end of the walk, we all got medals to hang around our necks.

The cherry trees are in beautiful bloom, so we took a moment off to admire them.

An hour or so before it was time to pack everything up, stuff it in the car, take it home, and unload it all, something happened that I wanted to share with you. A man I'd never seen before stopped by our booth. He glanced at Karen's sign, and then his eyes strayed to the pile of books on the end of the table. "Have you read all those books?" he asked me.

"I wrote all these books," I said.

"Really? My wife loves your books. She has every one of them."

Fran Stewart

I suggested he sign his wife up for Karen's newsletter. I hope she wins the free massage!

The next time you attend an outdoor charity event like this, as you're walking around admiring all the booths, chatting with the folks attending them, and signing up for (or possibly buying) something, remember my second paragraph up there, and understand how much work is involved. It was fun, but we all got home pooped.

BeeAttitude for Day #530: *Blessed are those who plan parks and who plant flowers in them for us to enjoy, for they shall see their work bloom.*

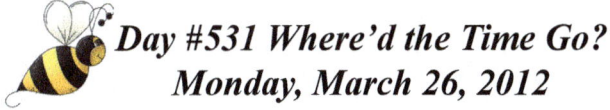 Day #531 Where'd the Time Go?
Monday, March 26, 2012

Where'd the time go?

When I started this blog, it seemed like 600 days would be so far in the future, I wouldn't have to worry about it. I thought those 600 days would take me through my first honey-harvest.

Well, if I still had the bees, I'm sure it would have.

I'm looking forward to the honey that will come from my bees, though, even if I'm not the one tending the hives. With the rate the weather's going around here, that should be fairly soon.

Speaking of weather, I found out why all this warm, unseasonable weather. Good old Science at NASA came up with this explanation about the solar eruptions that lit the thermosphere up "like a Christmas tree."

I thought you might be interested. I wonder if the bees are enjoying the results, or if they're getting too hot too soon.

https://science.nasa.gov/science-news/science-at-nasa/2012/22mar_saber/

BeeAttitude for Day #531: *Blessed are those who explain esoteric ideas, for they shall have the benefit of knowing they've enlightened others.*

[**2019 p.s.** Links are so awkward in a printed book. They worked just fine in the blog—and in the e-books—but there's simply no easy way to list them here. Sorry about that.

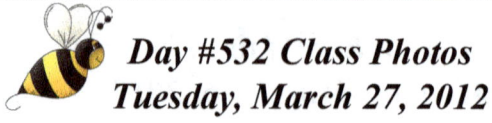
Day #532 Class Photos
Tuesday, March 27, 2012

I belong to Sisters in Crime. It's a nationwide organization for people who like mysteries. We all read them, some of us write them, and some sell them. There are a large number of librarians in the group, too.

We have a members-only online discussion forum, and a while back someone asked how do established authors choose names for their characters.

Good question.

Lots of people joined the discussion, and some of the talk centered around our own names—how often or how seldom we come across people with our own names.

The best post, though, came from Hank Phillipi Ryan, a well-established writer who mentioned a cartoon she'd seen in the New Yorker several years ago. It was drawn like a typical first grade class photo, with three rows of kids and a frumpy teacher.

The caption read:
  Mrs. Prohaska's First Grade Class:
- First row: Jennifer, Jennifer, David, Jennifer, David, David, Jennifer, Jennifer, David
- Second row: Jennifer, David, David, Mrs. Prohaska, Jennifer, David, David, Jennifer, Jennifer
- Third row: Jennifer, David, David, Jennifer, Jennifer, Jennifer

Were you ever in a class like that?
Just think of it. In a bee colony the class photo would read:

- First row: worker, worker, worker, queen, worker, worker, worker
- Second Row: worker, worker, worker, worker, drone, worker, worker
- Third Row: worker, drone, worker, worker, worker, worker, worker

BeesKnees #6: A Beekeeping Memoir

BeeAttitude for Day #532: *Blessed are those who continue to plant flowers, for they shall hear us humming all summer long.*

Day #533 How Many?
Wednesday, March 28, 2012

I used to try to count the number of bees in a square inch, or the number on top of the hive at any given time of day, or the number of bees along the top of a frame when I opened a hive.

Impossible.

Yesterday I had the same sort of problem trying to count the number of children at my granddaughter's birthday party. They kept wiggling. Shifting. Giggling and disappearing around the corner as they ran, laughed, played.

It was great fun. But I still have NO idea what the count was.

Then again, does the number really matter? Wasn't the laughter the important factor, not how many were laughing?

Gotta get my priorities straight.

BeeAttitude for Day #533: *Blessed are those who let us laugh in our own way, for they shall be more settled in their souls.*

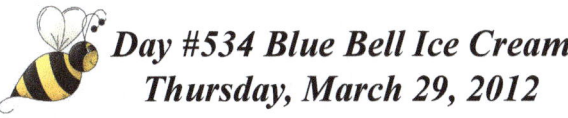 Day #534 Blue Bell Ice Cream
Thursday, March 29, 2012

In a comment on yesterday's blog post, Petie Ogg mentioned that not only will she be 18 years free of cancer this coming Sunday, but her family will be celebrating with Blue Bell Homemade Vanilla Ice Cream. Good for you, Petie!

Picture from Blue Bell's website

Her comment brought back an elusive memory—elusive in that I hadn't thought about it in maybe 20 years. I do wonder if my kids remember it – I'll have to ask them.

You may recall that I used to live in Vermont. And I used to be active in volunteering for the Vermont Public Television Auction. One year, one of the local businesses donated two five-gallon tubs of Blue Bell Ice Cream. One of Vanilla and one of Chocolate.

We bid on both of them, hoping to win one or the other.

We WON both of them.

Now, the only way to eat a 5-gallon tub of Blue Bell Ice Cream is to sit it on the floor, get a long-handled spoon for everyone in the family, and dig in.

We even got to where we'd let guests in on the game. The ones who took us up on it were the true friends indeed.

BeeAttitude for Day #534: *Blessed are those who celebrate with joy, for their hearts shall be light.*

Day #535 Citizen Fire Academy Class #3: the 911 Center
Friday, March 30, 2012

Thursday evening we were at the Gwinnett County 911 Center for the third class in the Gwinnett Citizen Fire Academy.

The first half of the class we learned a great deal about the operations of the 911 center, how the 911 operators are trained, what the backup systems are in case of a power failure, and how the center responds to heavy emergencies, such as the floods that hit Gwinnett County in September of 2009 or the day Brian Nichols escaped from a local courthouse, killing people in the process.

We heard about the high turnover rate. Many people just can't remember the codes, or they'll freeze up when there's a real emergency. Many others find they simply can't take the pressure.

We saw the plaques on the wall citing the 911 operators who had either saved a life or delivered a baby. Yes, that's what I said – delivered a baby – i.e. talked a person through the process when they called 911 in a panic.

For the second half of the class, we had a chance to wander around and speak with the various operators. I ended up listening to Melissa as she fielded calls. When she wasn't answering a call, she took time to explain to me the 4-computer-monitor system she has to keep track of.

Seconds after I took this photo, she was answering, "911. Where is the location of your emergency?" 911 operators have to memorize hundreds of codes so they can key in the calls quickly and efficiently.

During another of her brief respites, I asked if she'd ever delivered a baby. Her face lit up. "Sometimes," she said, "people can work here for ten years and never get a childbirth call, but I've only been here a year, and I've already delivered one!"

I asked how she did it, and she showed me the card file (written by a medical doctor) that walks the operators through the exact questions to ask.

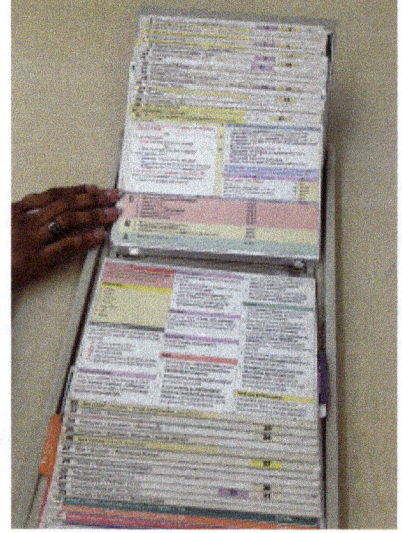

Here's the first section of the Childbirth Card:

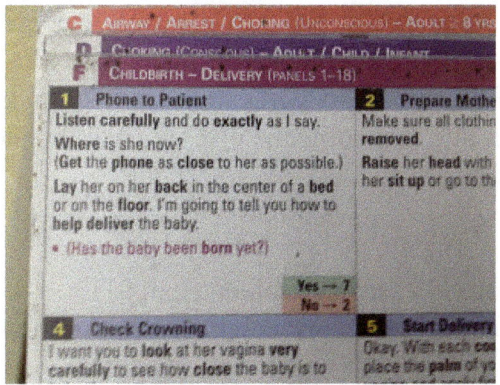

"Did you use this card?" I asked her.

"I SURE DID!" was her answer.

And now her name with be on the 2012 plaque! Makes me proud that I talked with her.

I also asked Melissa if she saw this job as a long-term career, or would she go on to something else in a year or two. "Oh, no! I wouldn't leave. This is the most wonderful job in the world. Where else could I be so challenged to do my best? I never know who's going to be on the other end of a call."

My best advice to you after having seen the 911 center:

Learn the **non-emergency** phone number of your local 911 center.
In Gwinnett County GA, it's 770-513-5700
Program it into your speed-dial

- If you see someone driving erratically, but there's no accident, get the license plate and call the non-emergency number.
- If you hear a gunshot in your neighborhood, but have no idea where it came from, call the non-emergency number.
- If you've lost your wallet (or you find a wallet), call the non-emergency number.

- If your neighbor's barking dog is driving you nuts, call the non-emergency number.

Those are all important calls, but they are NOT emergencies, and will be answered as soon as an operator is available (one who is not handling an emergency). Remember—if you call 911 without a true emergency, you're tying up a line that someone else in a life-threatening situation truly needs.

But:
- If that driver causes a serious accident, call 911
- If the gunshot comes from your neighbor's house and you hear someone scream, call 911. In fact, if you hear somebody scream, even if you don't know which house it is, call 911.
- If the lost wallet is attached to a dead body, call 911.
- If that dog attacks someone and you see it, call 911.

And if you're driving down the road and your baby starts to make its way into the world, pull off to a safe place and call 911. They'll dispatch an ambulance; but, if necessary, they can talk you through the delivery.

That's nice to know, isn't it?

BeeAttitude for Day #535: *Blessed are those who welcome a job that involves challenge, for they shall glow with a feeling of accomplishment when their workday is ended. We bees end every day like that.*

BeesKnees #6: A Beekeeping Memoir

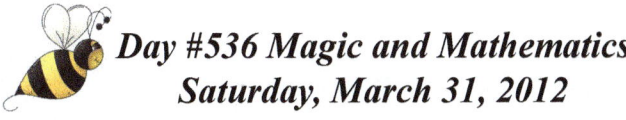
Day #536 Magic and Mathematics
Saturday, March 31, 2012

Magic and Mathematics were stunningly combined this weekend at the Gathering for Gardner in Atlanta. I was fortunate enough to have been invited to attend the Friday evening dinner and magic show.

Martin Gardner was a man fascinated by mathematics. Although he was never trained professionally as a mathematician, he popularized math, puzzles, and sleight of hand, bringing—as Richard K. Guy has said—"more mathematics, to more millions, than anyone else."

This logo for the Gathering for Gardner was designed by Scott Kim. Notice how the letters are made up exclusively of the numbers zero through nine. Just seeing the logo was worth the journey into Atlanta on a rainy night.

And the show after dinner? Fantastic! Every single act was wonderfully entertaining. People telling jokes, doing magic tricks with cards, miming the meeting between a young woman and a "worm" made of squashy aluminum air conditioning duct stuff, and a twelve-year-old (**Ethan Brown**) who could do square roots and cube roots in his head. Look him up and you can see him at age ten wowing various science conferences.

Fran Stewart

The final act was of a strong man in the tradition of the old strong men of the vaudeville circuit. Dennis Rogers bent nails, tore phone books apart, bent a socket wrench, wrenched apart a horseshoe, and deflected a bowling ball dropped onto his stomach from a the top of an 8' ladder. There's a YouTube video out there of him straightening out a horseshoe.

Was I astonished? Yes. Was I delighted? Absolutely. But even more than that, it was great fun being in a ballroom full of people for whom math is fun.

BeeAttitude for Day #536: *Blessed are those who can be surprised, for they shall find endless entertainment around them.*

Day #537 Bees Invade Congress
Sunday, April 1, 2012

In a surprise move, a group of politically active honeybees invaded the U.S. Senate and House of Representatives early this morning. They installed Queen Bees in the positions of leadership, knowing full well that the queen bees haven't much to do with how the hive is ordered.

Drones rearranged the furniture and seated all the workers alphabetically (Worker A, Worker B, Worker C, and so on), rather than the outdated two-party system (I'm on this side of the aisle and you can't make me see your point of view because you're on the other side).

After only a few hours in control, bees have banned pesticides and herbicides, made high-fructose corn syrup illegal, arranged tax incentives for people with home gardens, and arranged for free honeycomb samples for schools across the nation.

"We work together," the Queen Bee of the Senate told a large gathering of media this morning. "Now, please excuse me. We all have to get back to work."

Stay tuned for regular updates on the new State of BEEunion.

BeeAttitude for Day #537: *Blessed are those who eat honey, for they shall be bright-eyed.*

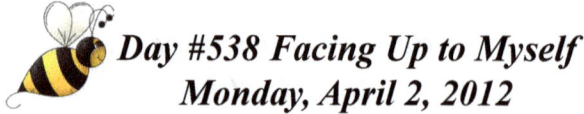

Day #538 Facing Up to Myself
Monday, April 2, 2012

A number of years ago I developed a severe allergy to eye make-up, and at the same time, the foundation I wore started making me itch. After that happened, all I had was my face, without the facade I'd been using. I was haunted on the inside, and the allergy made me "face up" to who I really was and what I was doing (or wasn't doing) with my life. Looking back, it was the best thing that ever happened to me. At the time, though, it felt devastating.

I had a home-based business selling cosmetics. I won't tell you which brand, but think pink. I was doing well at it.

I got up each morning, cleansed my face, moisturized, layered on foundation, blush, eyeliner, two (or three) shades of shadow, mascara (brown first, then tip the lash ends with black), lip liner and lipstick.

Each evening I reversed the process, removing it all and moisturizing like crazy.

I did this even if I had nowhere to go except to take out the garbage.

One of the women in my sales unit, though, used no makeup whatsoever, except a little lipstick occasionally. She gave a speech once at a sales meeting in which she said that the skin care routine was enough for her because, essentially, she liked who she was and what she was doing with her life. "I feel completely comfortable in my skin," is how she put it.

I remember being silently critical. You're dowdy. You could look so much better with a little blush and eyeliner and shadow and ... How stupid I was. If I'm honest with myself, I also felt a twinge of envy that any woman could be so ... so content. Her peaceful face infuriated me, because I could see no possibility of such peace in my own life.

I'm not saying that everyone who wears makeup has an unfulfilled life. Not at all. But I wish it hadn't taken me so many years (and that allergic reaction) to wake up to my own possibilities.

BeeAttitude for Day #538: *Blessed are those who know the wonders they are capable of, for they shall rise each morning with enthusiasm, excitement, and expectancy, just the way we bees do.*

Day #539 Terri Caught a Swarm
Tuesday, April 3, 2012

I met Terri Tattan when she organized (and I helped staff) a beekeeper's display at Whole Foods, where Terri works. She became interested in beekeeping, joined our club, and is a stalwart member now.

Whole Foods has an observation hive, a beautifully built glass-sided, rotating hive that has a very L-O-N-G tube to the outside of the store. The bees come and go all day long.

Well, a few days ago the bees swarmed. Terri ran home, got her beekeeper's suit, and captured the swarm right out of the Whole Foods parking lot.

I'm happy to report that the bees are still with her, and appear to be happy in their new home. Congratulations on your first swarm-capture, Terri!

BeeAttitude for Day #539: *Blessed are those who help us find good homes, for they shall receive the extra honey we make.*

Day #540 Specialized or Multifaceted?
Wednesday, April 4, 2012

One of the disadvantages of technology is the increasing specialization, in which one expert's field of study is so narrow, there seems to be no connection to anything outside of that field.

Bees don't have that problem. In the course of a worker bee's life, she will perform every single job in the hive except laying eggs. She does each job for a few days until she graduates to the job of foraging, and that's the job she'll hold until she dies. Every bee is, therefore, multifaceted.

I know we can't expect human society to work that way, but sometimes, I have to think it might be nice.

Why am I thinking this way? Well, not to belabor a point, but I've been experiencing a certain structural problem in my innards. Monday I went to my regular family doctor—someone I don't visit very often because I'm amazingly healthy. But everyday life has become extremely uncomfortable for me, and I figured it was time to do something about it.

"You need to see a urologist," he said, based on what I told him of what I was experiencing. So he recommended someone, I called, and they said, "We can get you in tomorrow morning at 9:45."

Tuesday I went to the urologist – a very decent guy who has the kind of job everyone jokes about, but I was grateful for his patience and gentleness. He explained every step of the way. Finally he told me that I was mistaken. The problem was not what I had thought it was. Everything was fine in my insides as far as his field of expertise went. My problem wasn't related to urology. I needed to see a gynecologist.

He recommended one, I called, and made an appointment for next week.

I'm genuinely hoping that this is the last doc I'll need to see about getting this problem taken care of. Either that or I need to sprout bee-wings so I never have to sit down again.

On the other hand, if I need someone's expertise, I'm really glad it's available.

And, while I'm thinking of happy thoughts:

Happy Birthday, Aiden!

BeeAttitude for Day #540: *Blessed are those who take the time to bee gentle, for they shall bee appreciated.*

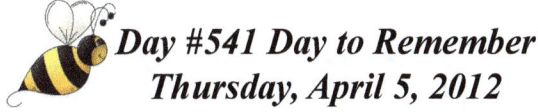 Day #541 Day to Remember
Thursday, April 5, 2012

Do you ever have those days when all you seem to do is spin your wheels?

I doubt that ever happens to bees, unless they're trapped inside the hive because of day after day of rainy weather.

That's what Wednesday has been like for me (as I write this sometime after 11 pm on the 4th). I probably should have packed the car for my book signing at The Principal's Palette, a gift store in Winder GA. That will be Thursday evening from 4:30 to 7:00. Instead I've left it off until the last minute. Phooey.

I did get some writing done, but then I re-read it and decided about half of it was absolute blather. Thank goodness for the delete key.

Then, about 10pm I took out the CD I'd picked up from Wolf Camera. I've had 200 and some-odd slides in a metal box stuffed in the back of a closet for years. Last week I took them to Wolf and said, "Can you put these on a CD for me?"

"Yes ma'am," they said. "That'll be $165 please."

Ah well, it was bits and pieces of my childhood on film after all, so I paid them, and picked up the final product on my way to the Silver Sneakers class Wednesday.

I just spent about an hour looking at them. Was my mother ever that young? Was my father ever that virile-looking? Were my sister and I ever so silly together? Well, I can believe that last one, since we still are!

Instead of thinking of all this as just spinning my wheels, I'm going to call today a day to remember.

BeeAttitude for Day #541: *Blessed are those who can recall their past with joy, for they shall have smiles in abundance.*

Day #542 The Principal's Palette
Friday, April 6, 2012

This post has nothing to do with bees.

The first Thursday of each month is a special time at The Principal's Palette Gallery, a gift shop, art store, and handcraft haven in Winder GA. On that day each month, proprietor Lynn Hammond invites local (and sometimes not so local) artists, crafters, or writers to showcase their work.

[**2019 Note**: I hate to keep having to say that businesses have gone out of business, but The Principal's Palette is yet another one that folded several years ago, which is why I've not included a website link.]

I was there talking about my books last night, and had great fun meeting people. Debra Gilstrap was there, too, showing her handcrafted jeweled eggs, in perfect time for Easter.

And, as always at my book signings, I had with me some copies of my sister's book Depression Visible: the Ragged Edge. You just never know when the subject will come up. When it does, I don't particularly care whether or not I sell any of my own books if there's a chance to give hope. I'm gratified that there now is someone who will be able to understand what depression is, what it means to the person who is affected by it, how it affects the entire family/friend structure around that person.

If you haven't checked out the Diana Alishouse website (depressionvisible.com), you might want to give it a try. You might not need it yourself, but someone you know might truly appreciate finding out about it.

There is hope. There is help available. But for that to happen, the depression needs to be visible, to be recognized. Diana's book can help.

BeeAttitude for Day #542: *Blessed are those who plant native shrubs, flowers, and trees, for they shall help to promote local honey production.*

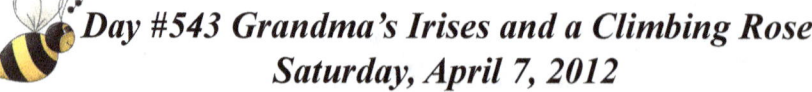 Day #543 Grandma's Irises and a Climbing Rose
Saturday, April 7, 2012

Wanted to share with you some of what's going on in my yard.

Last year I planted a climbing rose and thought I'd have a couple of years before I needed to build a trellis for it to climb on. Not so. Many of the shoots are eight feet long, drooping into the narrow walkway that goes around that side of the house.

A couple of days ago I walked out the front door and just happened to look to my left. This is what I saw, one lonely but BRIGHT bloom.

Up closer, it looks like this:

Then there are my grandmother's irises. I think I've mentioned before that she had an iris garden on the farm in Mississippi.

[**2019 Note:** See the baby sassafras tree with the mitten-shaped leaves branching out just behind this iris? The squirrels must have planted it. I certainly didn't. But now it's tall enough and full enough to shade my front porch in the morning so I can sit there in comfort to drink my tea even during the heat of the summer.]

When Grandma died forty years ago, my Aunt Mary dug up half of the irises and transplanted them into her own garden, where they grew with abandon.

Every time Aunt Mary moved, she'd dig up half the irises and take them along with her.

I visited her in Tennessee a dozen years ago and brought back two big boxes of them. When I moved to this house—well, you get the idea.

The point to all this is that in each of these moves, there were irises left behind that then continued to multiply. My grandmother's irises have populated dozens of gardens over the years – and I'm sure they're all still going strong.

Tomorrow I'll show you some of the other flowers I've carried along with me from one house to another.

BeeAttitude for Day #543: *Blessed are those who plant gardens wherever they go, for their work shall be revered by future homeowners and by us bees, too!*

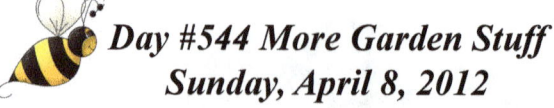 Day #544 More Garden Stuff
Sunday, April 8, 2012

Speaking of moving plants from one house to another, as I did in yesterday's post, when I first moved to Georgia twenty years ago I found a dianthus called Bath's Pink. It had been found and propagated by horticulture genius Jane Bath, and I bought a couple of pots of it when I visited her greenhouse.

The patch of it I transplanted to my current front yard seven years ago started out about three feet from the driveway. Then Panther, the only outdoor cat I've ever had (all the rest have been strictly indoor) decided that sleeping in the middle of the dianthus was a great way to spend a sunny day.

The middle of the patch pretty much disappeared, and what was left of the plant crept farther away from Panther's resting place, eventually spreading out onto the driveway. I'm not sure how it happened, but a layer of dirt accumulated underneath the sprigs of dianthus, and the plant took off. It likes growing on top of the concrete apparently. I strung an old garden hose around the area to delineate it, filled in with compost and mulch, and simply drive around it to get into the garage.

While I don't recommend planting over concrete, if you have a lovely flowering plant that thrives in what you think is a strange place, you might want to let it grow and see what happens.

That's how I ended up with all these wild asters. At least, that's what I think they are. If you know what they are for sure, please let me know. The bees like them. That's what counts for me.

BeesKnees #6: A Beekeeping Memoir

BeeAttitude for Day #544: *Blessed are those who keep their hands to themselves when visiting a beehive, for they shall enjoy the music of calm bees.*

Fran Stewart

 *Day #545 From the Sublime to the Ridiculous*
Monday April 9, 2012

All this weekend I've seemed to rotate between the divine and the drudgery, from the sublime to the ridiculous.

The divine was the bird song (and hums, too—the first hummingbird of the season!), the bluebird eggs that I took a peek at in the bluebird house, the teeny raccoon who wandered onto my front porch just as dusk was settling in (much to the delight of Daisy, who watched it quietly through the screen door), and the iris bud that over the past few days has been opening gradually. Here are some pictures of the process. Please keep in mind that my camera has its own idea about colors. The iris is not pink, not lavender. It's a deep, gorgeous, purply blue.

And then there was the drudge stuff. That's too strong a word. I actually enjoy the APA editing I do for doctoral dissertations. I get to read a wide variety of papers on a multitude of topics. But I'm working with a new client, and was unfamiliar with the advising professor's way of making comments on the paper.

My client, the doctoral candidate, sent me page after page of those comments to go along with the dissertation final draft (all ready for editing). Yikes! Here's a tiny section of those comments:

AWKWARDLY WRITTEN – REVISE
BE SPECIFIC IN WHAT THEY FOUND
THIS PART OF THE SENTENCE NEEDS TO LINK TO HOPE AS WELL – OR ELSE IT JUST HANGS THERE AND IS VAGUE
"OF THE STUDY" – REMEMBER TO BE AS SPECIFIC AS POSSIBLE IN YOUR WRITING AT EVERY OPPORTUNITY
WHAT TYPE OF GOALS? ACADEMIC ACHIEVEMENT?
CASUAL LANGUAGE
WHAT DID THEY FIND SPECIFICALLY?
THIS IS DATED INFO I BELIEVE – CHECK AND SEE WHAT MC COMPETENCE ASSESSMENTS HAVE COME OUT IN THE 8 YEARS AFTER THIS

I thoroughly dislike anything written in all capital letters. I don't like being shouted at—either in person or in writing. At any rate, it's very late, and I've taken a break. After I get this blog entry posted, I'm going to go sit on my front porch and listen to the night sounds for a while.

I'll be back at the dissertation tomorrow (including all those shouting caps-lock COMMENTS) – but for now: cricket sounds!

BeeAttitude for Day #545: *Blessed are those who stop to listen occasionally, for they shall be surprised at how much they hear.*

p.s. Today would have been my dad's 97th birthday. He was a wonderful man, and I'm proud to be one of his daughters.

Day #546 How to Treat Adult Children
Tuesday, April 10, 2012

I shared with you a month or two ago the anguish of having my niece going through a life-threatening situation when a blood vessel broke in her brain.

I'm happy to report that Erica is home from the hospital, and is doing well.

I spoke with my sister yesterday, though, and found that she was going through some sort of withdrawal. I asked her to write about the experience so I could share it with you.

= = = = = = = = = =

How to Treat Adult Children by Diana Alishouse—April 2012

My adult daughter recently spent 32 days in a brain trauma unit in a hospital recovering from an aneurism. I spent hours and days with her—holding her hand, smoothing her hair, talking to her even (especially) when she was unconscious, grateful for her whispered word "Mommie." I listened to the conferences among the neurologists, surgeons, pulmonologists, acute care nurses, respiratory therapists, pharmacists, physical therapists, and case managers, learning and asking questions which they tried to answer in lay terms. Love and fear were constant. Adrenaline poured through my body.

After she was released I took her to her home and stayed there with her for a week while she recovered strength enough to walk and made arrangements for home-health care nurse visits and appointments with her regular doctor. I did the laundry, grocery shopping, and cooking. I fed the cats and cleaned their litter boxes and her house. I goaded her to do her exercises. Her tracheostomy wound was healing nicely and she got stronger and better each day. Friends came to visit and volunteered to take her to further doctor appointments until she could drive. I began to relax.

I was no longer needed, so I went home—hoping she wouldn't fall, hoping she would remember to take her medicines, hoping her friends wouldn't let her down. My intensive mothering job was done.

Then the adrenaline stopped and so did I. I slept. Now three weeks later I am still sleeping a lot and crying often as I slowly release the fear from my brain and my body.

There are millions of stories like this. Millions of mothers who instantly snap back to the mothering mode we enjoyed when our children were young. It takes its toll on us, but we are willing to do it. At some level, conscious or not, we enjoy babying our child again. But we must be willing to let go of it when the time is right.

I have realized that my sleeping and weeping is only partly because of the adrenaline let down. The other part is in letting go of the mothering of my "baby," that adult child of mine. And this realization reminds me of the mothering I received as the adult daughter of my mother and my mother-in-law—two very different people with very different styles.

My mother, Tommie, never understood that her role had changed when I became an adult. To her I was the ever wayward child whose independence was a source of sorrow to her. Her attempts at control of my choices and beliefs only pushed me away. She never understood that. She felt rejected despite my many attempts to reassure her that I loved her still, although I disagreed with her. I could never love her enough.

My mother-in-law, Lennie, saw all of us, sons, daughters and in-laws, as adults. Quietly, she disagreed with many of our ideas, beliefs, and actions. She never pressed an issue or argued—only shook her head and kept on loving us. She was greatly loved.

==========

If you choose to share Diana's words with a friend who could benefit from them, please be sure to give Diana full credit.

BeeAttitude for Day #546: *Blessed are those who care for others, the way we bees take care of our young, for they shall see them flourish, and thrive, and fly.*

BeesKnees #6: A Beekeeping Memoir

 **Day #547 Iris and Docs**
Wednesday, April 11, 2012

Tuesday was the third doctor's appointment I've had in 8 days. At all three places, one or two people said, "Do you really not take any medications?"

When I said, "That's right! I don't!" they asked if I knew how unusual I was. I felt like a dinosaur – but a very healthy dinosaur.

I'm kinda pooped after that third appointment. It wasn't that awful; I was simply carrying around some tension about the whole process.

Not something I want to talk about in a public forum like this. Suffice it to say I'll be having surgery in a couple of months. When the doc said I couldn't lift anything for four to six weeks after the surgery, my reply was, "Then the surgery has to wait until I'm finished with the Gwinnett Citizen Fire Academy."

There's no way I'm going to miss getting into all that gear and going through the fire simulations.

In the meantime, enjoy this iris from my front yard:

BeeAttitude for Day #547: *Blessed are those who like to eat honeycomb, for they shall bee healthy indeed.*

 Day #548 Pen Women Nature Garden at Stone Mountain
Thursday, April 12, 2012

Yesterday I spent several relaxing hours at the Pen Women Nature Garden, which is nestled up against the base of the monolithic Stone Mountain, a few miles outside of Atlanta.

Monolith comes from two words that mean *one* (mono) and *stone* (lith). And one big stone it certainly is.

A year or so ago (on Day #176), I blogged about a hike I took around the base of Stone Mountain (just 2 weeks before I picked up my bees). This visit was much more relaxing. If you look at that blog post, you'll see how few leaves there were on the trees at the time. Now, 53 weeks later, you can see what an early spring we've had this year—so much so, that you can't see much of the mountain in these photos.

The April meeting of the National League of American Pen Women/Atlanta Branch is always held at our nature garden. *[2019 Note: We changed a couple of years ago to hold the October meeting at Stone Mountain.]* There, stepping stones (each with the name of an Atlanta Pen Women member) attest to the highly motivated writers, artists, and musicians who have belonged to our branch over the years. The garden was established in 1961 - and we had our 50-year celebration last year.

BeesKnees #6: A Beekeeping Memoir

This year I took dozens of photos, but will share only a few. Here's the start of the winding trail down to the garden from the parking area.

A bend in the trail:

I took a picture of a luscious patch of a native plant that grows alongside the trail and provides fruit for the birds, but decided not to put that photo in here. After all, it's *toxicodendron radicans,* otherwise known as poison ivy. Don't go walking off the path!

First part of the garden, just across a little bridge:

A gentle bend in the stone path:

My stone:

That dark mark under the quill (the emblem that means I'm a Letters Member) came from a wet fallen leaf that I brushed off the stone before I took the photo. Should have waited for it to dry. Or left the leaf there.

[**2019 Note:** I've added another membership category. I'm now a Music Member as well, based on a number of songs I've written, but I don't need to add musical notes to my stone. It's enough just to know where I stand.]

A nearby tree at the base of the monolith:

Don't you love those roots?

BeeAttitude for Day #548: *Blessed are those who plan beautiful places for the future, for they shall be praised by those who come after.*

Fran Stewart

Day #549 Citizen Fire Academy Class #4
Friday, April 13, 2012

Just so you'll know – I've decided not to quit my writing career to become a firefighter.

I came close to flunking Thursday evening when we had to don all the PPE (Personal Protective Equipment), including a 40-pound SCBA (Self Contained Breathing Apparatus). But, I did make it through the burned-out training building, holding onto someone's arm because I couldn't wear my glasses with that face mask on, and couldn't see a blinkin' thing.

I wasn't quite in panic mode, but close to it. I am such a wimp. So they took me back to the starting point and helped me take off the mask and air tank. Then, when I stopped hyperventilating, I joined the rest of the group.

But, I'm getting ahead of myself. This was our first view of the Gwinnett County Fire Academy Burn Building:

Then we went inside a different building to get into our gear.

Trevor had his on already,

so I handed him my camera:

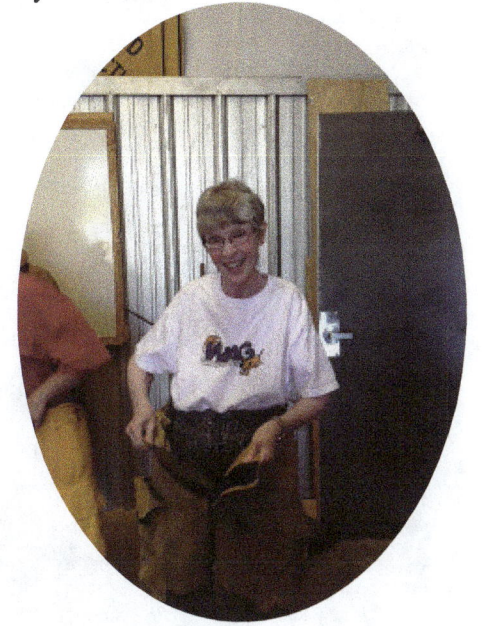

That coat alone is HEAVY, but if I were in a burning building with a temp between 400 and 1,200 degrees, I should think I'd appreciate all the protection I could get. As you can see, the top of the pants came nowhere near my waist, so the next step was the bright red suspenders (no picture of that).

Then we learned how everything went on properly, and watched as one of the instructors showed us how to do it right, so we could make it through the obstacle course.

One of the people helping us was Senior Fire Investigator Wade Crider, who told me he'd help me get my arson facts right for BROWN AS FUDGE, the next mystery in the Biscuit McKee Series. [**2019 Note:** The book turned out to be GRAY AS ASHES, which made more sense, because of its having arson as one of the major factors in the mystery. And a further note: Wade Crider died several years ago of mesothelioma, a pernicious cancer that is caused by asbestos inhalation. Unfortunately, it's something many fire investigators are subjected to, since they have to go into burned buildings that may have been built when asbestos was still used as an insulating material.]

We didn't have to go over the stones shown here or through the barrels – thank goodness. Imagine crawling through one of these, hauling a fire hose, with more than 40 pounds of clothing and gear.

Then we got to watch four of the Fire Explorers go through a training run. The Fire Explorers are young people between the ages of 14 and 19, who "explore" what it means to be a firefighter. The young woman on the right was accepted into the Fire Academy, by the way, and she'll start as a new recruit next Monday. As dusk descended, the markings on their uniforms really began reflecting the light.

BeesKnees #6: A Beekeeping Memoir

They stood at attention and, when the instructor said, "Go," they donned all their PPE in 46 seconds. I couldn't take pictures fast enough. The hood, the boots and pants, the snaps, the buckles, the Velcro, SCBA with strapping and air hoses, helmet, and gloves, and hands up in the air to show they'd finished. When I donned my SCBA, it took two minutes and two other people to help me get it up. These Fire Explorers threw their unit up and over their heads, where it settled onto their backs. Very impressive they were. The young woman finished first, incidentally. No wonder they recruited her.

Then they had to pick up a fire hose, climb through a 20" x 20" opening and over an A-shaped obstacle, through a tunnel, pick up the victim (a bundle of fire hose wrapped in pink, in the rough shape of a human body, with arms and legs dangling), and return with the "body" the way they came.

Like I said, I'm not gonna give up my writing job.

Next week: ladders!

p.s. Stop by your neighborhood fire station sometime soon and thank the people there.

BeeAttitude for Day #549: *Blessed are those who guard the hive, for they shall be appreciated by the rest of us bees.*

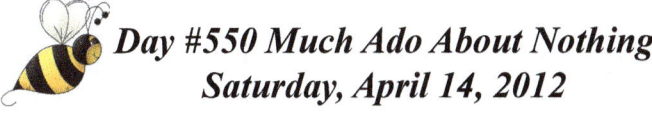 Day #550 Much Ado About Nothing
Saturday, April 14, 2012

Friday night I took one of my grandsons, the 12-year-old, to the New American Shakespeare Tavern to see Much Ado About Nothing, which just happens to be my very favorite Shakespearean comedy.

The Shakespeare Tavern is in the process of producing every single one of Shakespeare's comedies in the order in which they were written. Much Ado was the 7th of Willie's 12 comedies.

Seeing the familiar scenes and hearing the familiar words had an extra bit of magic as I saw Ethan absorb the wonder of it all.

If you don't live in the Atlanta area, and if you don't plan to visit in the next few weeks, there's a very good Kenneth Branagh / Emma Thompson movie of the play – but, all in all, I like the Tavern version better.

So much so, that I plan to see it again.

BeeAttitude for Day #550: *Blessed are those who give their best effort every time they fly, for they shall bring forth the best nectar.*

Day #551 Reel Mowers
Sunday, April 15, 2012

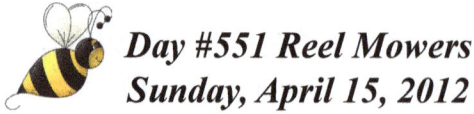

One of the loveliest sounds in my memory of childhood is the snip, snip, snip of lawnmowers on a Sunday afternoon as my dad tooled around the yard. Reel lawnmowers. The kind you push. The kind you don't have to turn on. The kind that doesn't take gas or electricity. The kind I have sitting in my garage.

There's a "reel" adventure to mowing my yard. I don't have to wear earplugs, which means I can hear the squirrels scolding me for getting near "their" birdseed at the bottom of the feeder.

I can hear the rustling as a neighbor's cat bursts from underneath the Vinca major (which is in danger of taking over the whole yard) and heads over toward the Hydrangea quercifolia (oak leaf hydrangea) to hide there until I disappear.

I can hear the wind blowing through the trees above me.

Of course, I stop frequently to unstick the reel from the pines cones that get wedged in it. But that's okay. That way I get to look closer at the native red clover to see if any honeybees have found it yet. Any day now, I hope.

BeeAttitude for Day #551: *Blessed are those who move slowly through life, for they shall see wonders all around them.*

Day #552 White Tower Ghost
Monday, April 16, 2012

In the mid-1970s I went to London for five glorious days. One of the highlights of that trip was my visit to the Tower of London. I thoroughly enjoyed the tour led by a highly knowledgeable guide, and laughed at the tale of how well potatoes grew in the grassy moat during World War II -- "Probably due to the excellent fertilizer," said our guide after having just told us about how bodies were disposed of, from the 13th to the 18th century, when there was still water in the moat.

"Now, do wander a bit, and don't forget to view the Museum of Armour in the White Tower," he told us before ending the tour. The White Tower is the oldest structure in the Tower of London. Built near the end of the 11th century, at the time of William the Conqueror, the White Tower is a squarish structure with turret-like structures at each corner, which I remembered as being round but are actually square.

Photo Credit: Wikipedia

I wasn't that interested in the museum of armor (not even a metal suit that belonged to Henry VIII), but I dutifully took a stroll up one staircase, through a floor, up the same staircase to the next floor, and so on. Helmets, visors, pikes, staffs, maces, swords, and more. Way more than I cared to linger over, so I headed for the other staircase.

In order to keep tourists from pushing each other down the stairs (accidentally, of course), there was a system in place that designated one corner turret as the UP staircase and one as the DOWN. The stairs were a blunt triangle in shape, with landings at each floor and at the outer edge, where a wide slit in the thick wall allows people to see out and lets some daylight in.

I went down one flight, to the outside edge of the tower, down another flight to the landing where the door opened out from that floor. It was January, and there weren't many other tourists around, so I was quite alone. I had taken three or four steps down from that landing when I heard light footsteps running down the stairs from the floor above me. I pressed myself against the outer wall of the stairway, since I didn't want to be perched on the narrow inner edge of the stairs with someone rushing past me.

I looked back up to my left and saw a woman in a dark green, long, full-skirted dress with a touch of white at the neckline. Her dark brown hair was pulled back with a ribbon of some sort. I could see the wall in back of her ... right through her. She was laughing.

BeesKnees #6: A Beekeeping Memoir

She ran past me, stopped on the landing a few steps below, placed her hands on the base of the wide window opening, and looked out and down. She laughed again, and ran on down the circular stairs.

I wondered what she'd been looking at, so I went to the same opening, placed my hands where hers had been, and looked down into the courtyard. A young man stood there, still looking up, with the happiest grin on his face. He wore a russet colored full-sleeved top, a slouchy hat, a heavy belt that held a long knife.

As I watched in absolute wonder, he turned his gaze down toward the bottom of the White Tower turret, then disappeared as two nuns, present-day tourists, walked right through him. The nuns kept going, but the young man was gone.

Why am I telling you this story? Because I had lunch on Sunday with a family whose son is writing a school report on the Tower of London. His mother knew that I'd had this experience at the Tower, and asked if I would come to lunch with them and tell her son my story.

He said he'd read on the Internet about ghosts in the White Tower, so I went online to see what the cyber world had to say. No ghosts like mine, I'm afraid. All the ghosts mentioned online are either scary or pathetic, homicidal or headless, maniacal or horribly depressed.

I'd like to set the story straight. The people I saw were fresh and happy, vibrant and joy-filled. And at least 300-years dead. I don't know what they were doing hanging around there, but I am delighted ... honored even ... to have glimpsed a tiny moment in their lives.

BeeAttitude for Day #552: *Blessed are those who laugh wonderfully every day, for they shall last.*

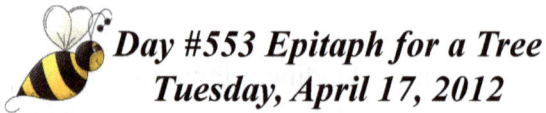
Day #553 Epitaph for a Tree
Tuesday, April 17, 2012

Monday, I said goodbye to an enormous pine tree. When I bought my house seven or eight years ago, the lowest branch of this particular pine was out of my reach. Over the years, though, the end of the branch seemed to droop lower and lower.

I finally figured out what was going on. The tree was leaning farther and farther to the east (and closer and closer to the power lines). Not a good idea.

I called the tree service folks who have done work for me before, and they quoted $550. But then, before I scheduled anything, I mentioned this to a friend of mine, and she said, "If it's leaning over the power line, call the electric company."

I did. They checked it out. And today, they took down the tree. Cost to me:
- zero dollars
- one oak leaf hydrangea that had the bad luck to have been planted (by me) underneath the lopsided pine, but which will, I'm sure, recover nicely
- some good-sized gouges in the ground
- two and a half hours of looking upwards, which resulted in a kink in my neck.

All in all, not a bad price to pay.

Here's the truck all set up at the end of my driveway:

By this time the guy in the bucket had taken off all the lower branches and was ready to cut down the top:

Another view of the bucket work after the tree's top had been removed:

Once they got to the point where the trunk was too large for the first saw, they changed to a chain saw. I managed to get this picture as the piece he'd just sawed off was falling to the ground.

Fortunately, I'd remembered to take down the bird nest on a pole nearby. The mama bird was a bit upset when her nesting box wasn't there (I'd put it on my front porch for safe-keeping), but she returned as soon as it was back in its place.

I didn't think I'd need to take down my bird feeder pole, though. I was far enough from the tree not to be in danger, right?

Let me tell you – those logs can bounce when they hit the ground. This big one came within a couple of feet of my bird feeders. Yikes! No harm done, fortunately.

And this log bounced and rolled about fifteen feet, right to the base of the tulip poplar, through the bed of Vinca major. Can you see that one pink rose back beside the house (out of the way, thank goodness)?

And this is what I was left with. The bedraggled plant on the right is what's left of the oak leaf hydrangea.

Incidentally, I asked them to leave the bottom 12 feet of the trunk intact. As it dies, there's a good chance a woodpecker will make a home in it. I hope so.

All is well. Thanks, Jackson Electric! And thanks for assuring me that there weren't any squirrel nests in the branches. Those critters may play havoc with my bird feeders, but I'd hate to destroy their houses.

BeeAttitude for Day #553: *Blessed are those who do their job in a workmanlike manner, for they shall have their praises sung by all us bees.*

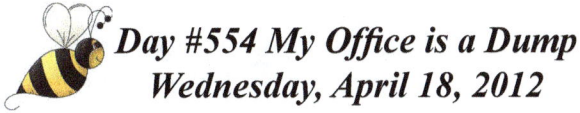 Day #554 My Office is a Dump
Wednesday, April 18, 2012

I'm almost ashamed to put this in writing – my office is a dump. Literally.

A number of months ago I had some people coming to my house for one of those jewelry shows. It was a fundraiser for the Gwinnett Choral Guild, which is the only reason I agreed to do it. In the course of cleaning up so I could make twelve women feel welcome in my minuscule living room, I collected a ghastly assortment of notebooks, pieces of paper, mail that wasn't immediately important, books, to-do lists…

I set them down on the floor of my office (since the tables were all – blush, blush – full). Then I closed the door and had a great party.

I booked another one. It was still benefitting the Choral Guild, after all.

This time—I don't know where it all came from—there were more of all the above categories, plus a few new ones. Boxes of mass market paperbacks of my books that came from World Wide Mystery (my m.m.p. publisher), more mail, some CDs, chargers for various electronic devices, plant lists, old beekeeper magazines.

Upstairs to my office. Put them on the floor next to the last stack(s).

After a while it was easier just to treat that room like a storage shed.

It's a dump. Once the jewelry shows were finished, I moved my computer down to the dining room. After all, this is where the bay window is, so I can work looking out at the woods behind the house.

I know there are probably some very important pieces of paper under those stacks. I'm sure of it. Can I find them, though? Nope. Might as well just pack everything in a few sturdy boxes and put them in the recycling bin.

Actually, my office is not a dump. The *upstairs storage shed* is a dump. My office, here with the birds flitting through the trees outside the bay window, is sheer heaven.

BeeAttitude for Day #554: *Blessed are those who make the most of the situation they're in, for they shall find nectar there somewhere.*

Day #555 A One-Year Retrospective
Thursday, April 19, 2012

A year ago I was in the middle of my first week with my bees. I still remember the excitement as I walked outside with a cup of tea each morning and sat beside the hives listening to the buzzing.

It was a precious time for me, maybe even more so in retrospect, as I now know that I can't have the bees there, that close to me. I've been re-reading my journal entries from last April, and I feel a lot like Emily Webb in Our Town. "Don't they even notice?" she wailed (or something like that – I'm remembering, not quoting exactly).

And no, I guess I didn't notice as much as I would have if I'd known I'd have those bees only a few short months. I loved them – but I would have loved them better if I'd known how soon they'd be gone.

I'm going to take a good look at my life. What are the things (or who are the people) I don't appreciate enough? What if they were gone tomorrow?

BeeAttitude for Day #555: *Blessed are those who pay attention, for they shall not miss out on the sweetness.*

Day #556 Fire Academy Class #5 - HOSE work
Friday, April 20, 2012

I lied. Last week I told you we'd be going up the ladders this week. Come to think of it, it wasn't really a lie. It was misinformation. We'll do ladders in class #7. This week we worked the fire hoses. Before class I had visions of myself in a cartoon-like event, flying around at the end of a runaway fire hose. It didn't happen like that, but there was a time (or two) when I felt like it might.

We were each issued a rolled-up 50-foot 2½-inch attack hose that we had to carry with us to each of the three "stations," and then the class was split into three groups. My group started out learning how to unroll the hoses and then how to roll them up two different ways depending on whether we'd be going into a house fire or a multi-story building fire.

By the time I'd rolled that sucker four or five times, I was pooped – and that station was the easy one.

For the second station, we had to wear our full turnout gear – pants, jacket, helmet, gloves. We learned how to get a "positive flow" of water from the fire hydrant to the fire truck so it would be available to the firefighters on the attack hoses (the ones that actually shoot the water onto the fire). Getting that positive flow meant lifting a 50-pound "water thief" – that's what they call it—don't ask me why—and setting it as close to the fire as possible. It's the red thing in the picture below. I couldn't lift it. The firefighter took pity on my wimpiness and picked it up for me.

Then, we had to open the hydrant to be sure we had a flow of clear water (no heavy sediments that might plug up the pumper truck). After that we attached a 5" yellow line from the hydrant to the fire thief and another one from the fire thief to the fire engine.

Turn it on slowly (to keep from bouncing the fire thief five feet up into the air) until the hose fills, then open it all the way. In the picture above, the hose from the hydrant to the Fire thief has filled, and the other one is about halfway full.

I won't even begin to try to explain all the pressure gauges and such that had to be watched, but the idea is to get the water from the hydrant into the pumper truck, which can then increase the pressure so the water will actually spray out of the end. Hydrants alone do not have enough pressure to drive much water through those hoses.

Suffice it to say that I managed to connect the couplings, open the hydrant, connect the hoses, and turn on the water. I needed help on opening the hydrant – there's a lot of friction in those connections. Twenty years ago I probably could have done it alone, but not this time.

Once we'd each had a chance to try all this, we went to the final station, where we got to advance a fire hose. The pressure on those suckers is enough to push someone over backwards, so, on my hands and knees, lugging the hose along with me, I crawled to the edge of the "burning building" (a grassy field beside the Fire Academy), and opened the nozzle very slowly. The person behind me was pushing against my back so I wouldn't be thrown backwards as I maneuvered the hose up and down, right and left (a sweep), and in a T (straight up, back and forth, then straight down the middle). Then we changed positions, so we could each experience both jobs.

We thought that was hard, but then we had a chance to hold the BIG hose used on huge fires. It had so much power, we had to coil it around in a loop and sit on the place where it crossed over. That fella pushes out 1,500 gallons per minute. I couldn't manage the hose by myself, so two firefighters positioned themselves on either side of me and helped me hold the hose (so I wouldn't kill anyone—I'm sure that was what their reasoning was).

I wish I had lots of pictures to share with you, but I took only a few. We were so busy, I didn't remember to click the button.

Suffice it to say that, with every class, my respect for the men and women who fight fires grows as fast as a fire does. Did you know a fire doubles in size every thirty seconds?

BeeAttitude for Day #556: *Blessed are those who teach others, for they shall leave the world a better place.*

p.s. Helmets are color-coded—I think I got this right, but I may have missed a color:

Blue = Citizen Fire Academy students and cadets
Black = Fire Academy personnel
Green = CERT members
Yellow = firefighters and drivers
Red = staff officers
White = the Fire Chief

Second BeeAttitude: *We bees do not have to bee color-coded. We know who we are and what we do.*

Day #557 Bees Are Taxed Fairly
Saturday, April 21, 2012

If you work for the IRS, I'd like to see you out of that job and into something that is less bureaucratic and more productive.

I went online some time ago to find a downloadable 1099 form – and this is a **small part** of what I was faced with:
= = = = = = = = = =
Available Products
In addition to these general instructions, which contain general information concerning Forms 1097, 1098, 1099, 3921, 3922, 5498, and W-2G, we provide specific form instructions as separate products. Get the instructions you need for completing a specific form from the following list of separate instructions.
  - Instructions for Forms W-2G and 5754
  - Instructions for Form 1097-BTC
  - Instructions for Form 1098
  - Instructions for Form 1098-C
  - Instructions for Forms 1098-E and 1098-T
  - Instructions for Forms 1099-A and 1099-C
  - Instructions for Form 1099-B
  - Instructions for Form 1099-CAP
  - Instructions for Form 1099-DIV
  - Instructions for Form 1099-G
  - Instructions for Form 1099-H
  - Instructions for Forms 1099-INT and 1099-OID
  - Instructions for Form 1099-K
  - Instructions for Form 1099-LTC
  - Instructions for Form 1099-MISC
  - Instructions for Form 1099-PATR
  - Instructions for Form 1099-Q
  - Instructions for Forms 1099-R and 5498
  - Instructions for Form 1099-S
  - Instructions for Forms 1099-SA and 5498-SA
  - Instructions for Forms 3921 and 3922
  - Instructions for Form 5498-ESA

See How To Get Forms, Publications, and Other Assistance on page 14.
= = = = = = = = = =

The explanations for each of those types of forms filled dozens of pages. Does it seem to you that this is just a wee bit complicated? Unnecessarily complicated?

We could learn something from the bees. They all work, they all produce something of value to the community, and they are "taxed" for their consumption (the honey and pollen they consume).

I kept seeing fairtax.org in the e-signature of a friend of mine and began to wonder what it was all about. So I went to the website, clicked on How Fair Tax Works, and listened to the video presentation. Next I clicked on FAQs and saw that there were all sorts of questions I could click on to see the answers. It took me a minute or two to figure out how the video works, but I found little white tabs on each side of the video box. When I clicked on them, I could move backward or forward through different topics, which seemed to correspond with the questions listed on the left, although the speaker's answers added to the written answers. I listened to a LOT of them, and liked what I heard (and read).

Seemed to me that the folks who put this idea together have taken a lesson or two from the bees.

BeeAttitude for Day #557: *Blessed are those who pay attention to us bees, for they shall gain insights they might have missed otherwise.*

[**2019 Note:** Have you noticed recently how complicated websites are getting? It seems like every time somebody thinks of a way they can stick in a link to give you just a little bit more information, they put it in there (cleverly concealed in one of dozens of dropdown menus) and send me wafting around cyberspace as I search for one or two arcane bits of information. I'd rather see a straightforward list of what's available, and then let me go where I want to without all the fancy-schmantzy graphics. Needless to say, I didn't go through all that fairtax maze this time around. There's a button on there for FAQ—good luck finding it. And they have webinars now. Check it out for yourself.]

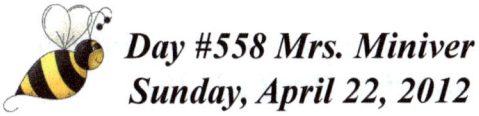 *Day #558 Mrs. Miniver*
Sunday, April 22, 2012

I wonder if bees buzz around in the evening after dark, recounting tales of what they did during the day, of how they found a new nectar source or drove a mouse from the hive, how they battled raindrops and survived by hiding under a Hosta leaf, or how they capped the latest batch of honey.

Chances are slim that they'd spend time telling war stories. That seems to be reserved for humans.

As I write this blog post, at 10:30 on Saturday evening, I just finished watching Mrs. Miniver, a 1942 movie starring Greer Garson and Walter Pigeon.

It's a story of the power of common people to rise above the horrors of war. It was written while a war still raged throughout Europe and the Pacific. I could remember my mother talking about it and what an inspiring movie it was. That alone (my mother's recommendation, that is) was enough to keep me from watching it for many years.

But then I got curious and ordered it from Netflix. I'm glad I did. For once, I can say my mama was right. I'm not sure how calm I'd be in a bomb shelter. I'm not sure how I'd face up to the loss of a family member. I'm not sure how I'd respond if my boat were required for another rescue at Dunkirk.

The value of a good movie is that it gives us a chance to ask those questions. And to pray that the need never arises to answer them.

BeeAttitude for Day #558: *Blessed are those who protect the hive, for they shall help a new generation of bees grow and flourish.*

This is Earth Day - Help Our Mother

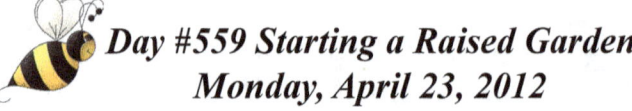 *Day #559 Starting a Raised Garden*
Monday, April 23, 2012

Home Depot had a raised-bed garden kit on sale a few days ago. Do you know how little room there is for a 4-foot square garden in my yard? Oh, there's plenty of room, but before I can use it, I have to rip out the EXTREMELY effective ground cover that I started eight years ago, when I thought I wouldn't want to mow much grass.

This morning I tackled an area right beside the front walk, in front of the birdbath and just downhill from the safflower-seed feeder. After an hour, this is what I had. Pretty pathetic, isn't it? Those are four-foot-long boards, by the way.

The other side of the path, the side with the Vinca major, looks great,

particularly the end that has the honeysuckle blooming in it.

But it may be a while before I can get the wild strawberry and Vinca minor pulled out. Wonder if it'll be too late to plant anything by the time I do???

BeeAttitude for Day #559: *Blessed are those who plan ahead, for they shall find the road easier. Maybe.*

[**2019 Note:** It took me a long time to figure out just how much of a thug plant that *Vinca major* was – and even longer to get it (almost) all pulled out by the roots. I'm still fighting it after seven years.]

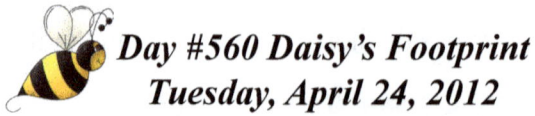 Day #560 Daisy's Footprint
Tuesday, April 24, 2012

When I bought this house almost eight years ago, it was in an "as is" state, which meant a great deal of it was fairly shoddy. Over the years I've replaced all the appliances, the furnace, the toilets, most of the faucets, and the water heater (my wonderful plumbers at Keep Smiling Plumbing love me).

I had to rip out ALL the carpeting because what was here was so filthy. Because I had a bunch of cats, though, I chose not to put in any new carpeting except in the one completely cat-free room in the entire house.

I probably should have replaced the linoleum that goes through the dining room and kitchen, but I decided that, with some elbow grease, I could put up with it for a few years. The other floors, the ones without linoleum, were just the bare sub-flooring, so I cleaned them all, bleached them, sealed them, and painted them various colors. I now have green floors upstairs, blue on the middle level, and a red floor downstairs.

Four years ago I decided to repaint the blue floor – it was getting worn in a number of places, and the white sealant was showing through.

So, I strung up chicken wire to keep the cats off the floor while it was drying.

Right.

That cruddy linoleum ended up with Daisy-footprints all across the width of the dining room.

I was almost finished cleaning them up, when it occurred to me that the one little footprint remaining might be kind of cute if I left it there.

So I did.

It's getting a bit worn, unfortunately, so I try to keep from stepping on it.

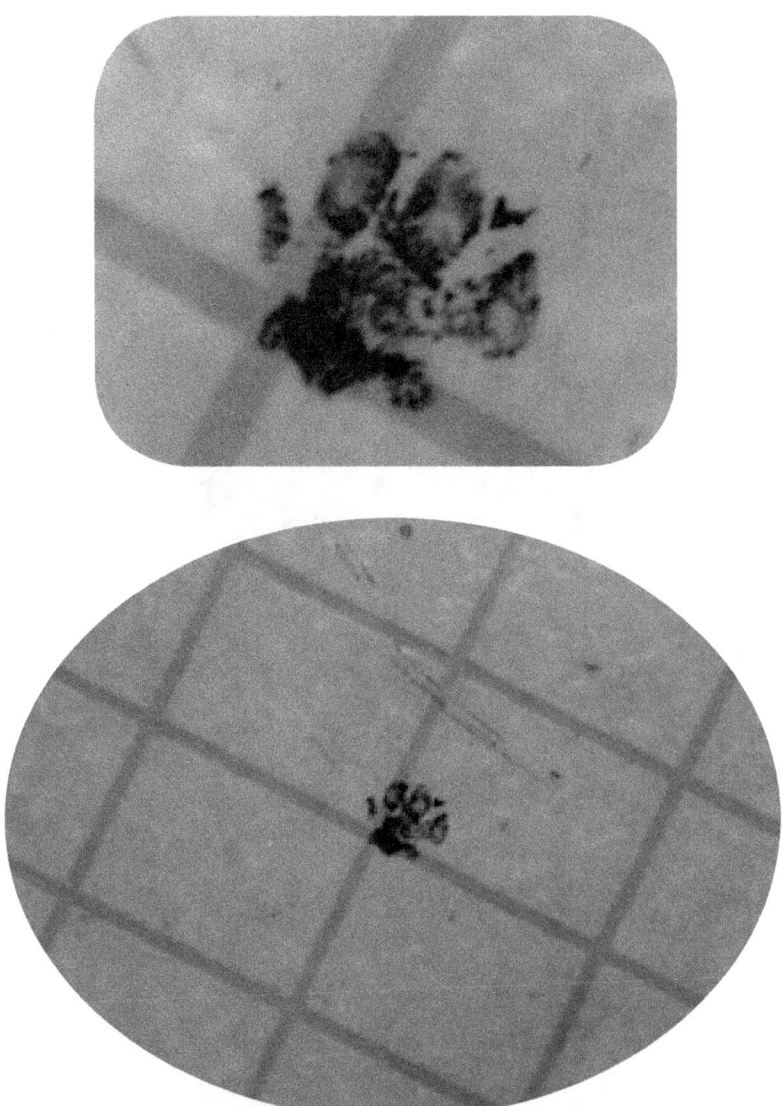

It covers about one square inch, and I laugh whenever I see it, so I thought I'd share it with you. See what I mean about the cruddy linoleum? Those scratches and the ground-in dirt have been there for eight years. They'll last a few more. After all, if I replace the flooring, I'll have to get rid of the footprint.

That would never do.

BeeAttitude for Day #560: *Blessed are those who don't bother to plan ahead, for they shall find surprises along the way.*

Day #561 Fat, Sick, and Nearly Dead
Wednesday, April 25, 2012

A friend of mine told me about a documentary movie called *Fat, Sick, and Nearly Dead.*

It's the story of Joe Cross, an Australian who was all three of those things. He came across the idea of drinking fruit and vegetable juices (and nothing else) for 60 days. This film is the story not only of what happened to him, but of how he inspired another man, a truck driver named Phil, to take responsibility for the shape his life was in.

Phil is the real star, and his journey from the brink of death to a radiant life is truly inspiring. If you have an hour and a half (even if it's spread across three days), you might want to watch it. You can find it at https://www.rebootwithjoe.com/joes-films/

BeeAttitude for Day #561: *Blessed are those who know where the pollen comes from – and who fly out to get it.*

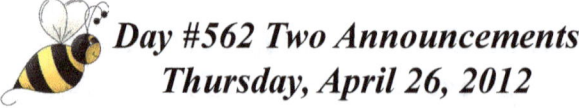

Day #562 Two Announcements
Thursday, April 26, 2012

The GOOD NEWS:
Just in case you're interested, here's a blurb about a writers workshop I'll be teaching next week at the Harris Arts Center in Calhoun, GA.

=========

Saturday May 5 from 10 am until 12 noon, award-winning author Fran Stewart will be signing *Violet as an Amethyst,* her new Biscuit McKee Mystery, and conducting Q & A session.

Mystery Writing Workshop 2:00 - 5:30 / $40
Join Fran Stewart as she teaches you how to polish your prose using colanders, stinky feet (not real ones), and avalanches as learning tools. This light-hearted interactive workshop is, in essence, a master's class for writers.

Fran will focus on one of the biggest problems that haunt most writers—how to make characters come alive. Using her writer's workbook, *From the Tip of My Pen*—a compilation of six years of monthly essays she wrote for the Atlanta Writers Club—Fran will lead you through easy-to-follow steps for writing effective dialogue and building dynamic characters.

=========

NOW, THE NOT SO GOOD NEWS:
And then there's the not-so-happy news. I've decided I need to drop out of the Citizens Fire Academy for now. I hope, after I have the surgery this summer, I'll gain a lot more energy and be able to pick up the last seven classes the next time around.

For now, though, I feel like I'm carrying around an anchor. As much as I've enjoyed the classes, my body simply isn't cooperating.

Happy Birthday, Savannah!

BeeAttitude for Day #562: *Blessed are those who fly as well as they can for as long as they can, for they shall find wonderful nectar. Blessed are they, also, who know their limits, for they shall find their nectar close to home.*

Day #563 Polly and the Honeybee
Friday, April 27, 2012

It was hard, turning in all my Citizen Fire Academy turnout gear last night. I gave everyone in the class a copy of one of my mass-market paperbacks – I had some promotional copies left over from the ones sent to me by World Wide Mystery. I'm not allowed to sell them, so I figured giving them to the class and the instructors would be a good idea.

A few days ago, Miss Polly settled in my lap and put her head under my hand. For sixteen years, she's known how to get a good scratch from a good scratcher when she sees one! My phone was sitting beside me so, one-handed, I managed this picture.

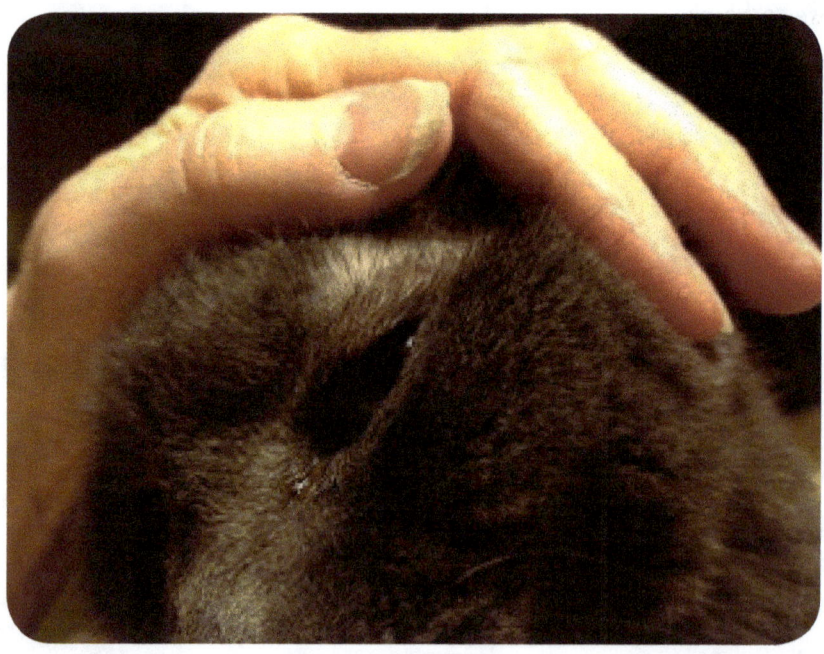

She spotted a honeybee on the outside of the picture window yesterday and spent several minutes watching it crawl around. The belly-side view is fascinating. I watched it with her. Wish I'd taken a picture, but this fuzzy photo from a previous blog post will have to suffice.

I'm gonna miss Miss Polly when she's gone.

BeeAttitude for Day #563: *Blessed are those who take the time to SEE what they're looking at, for they shall have wonders unfold before them.*

Day #564 A Spanish Course in Miniature
Saturday, April 28, 2012

The first Stella d'Oro Hemerocallis (day lily) bloomed a couple of days ago. These teeny little daylilies are the brightest gold. Only two blooms so far, but soon that corner of the yard will be filled with golden stars (which is what the name means in Spanish).

Speaking of Spanish, I don't know whether I've mentioned this yet, but I'm taking a Spanish language course. It's all on CDs, and I practice each morning for half an hour (1 track per day). This afternoon I ended up sitting in a medical office off and on for an hour and a half, having a repeat mammogram and then waiting for the results. One of the other women in the waiting room spoke Spanish, and I asked her a tentative question, figuring the worst she could do was ignore me. Instead, after a moment's surprise as she tried to figure out what I was saying, she smiled and answered my question very clearly, as if talking to a three-year-old.

I thanked her and said, in Spanish, "No hablo Espanol muy bien." *I don't speak Spanish very well.*

"Pero intiende," she said. *But you understand*

"No mucho," I replied, "no intiendo mucho. Pero …" and there I stopped. I didn't know the word for *I try*, so I said it in English with a questioning lift to my voice.

"Trato," she said.

"Si! Trato. Yo trato." Yes, I try. I try.

Now, keep in mind, I'm not learning how to SPELL Spanish – the course I'm taking is strictly conversational, so if I offend your superior Spanish language knowledge, feel free to teach me (gently, please) as to the correct spelling.

The important thing is that I reached out despite my reluctance to sound ignorant, and learned a new word out of it. I also received a lovely smile of delight from the woman with whom I tried to connect and whose language I tried to honor.

That felt good.

And the mammogram? It was absolutely negative. All is well on that end of things.

BeeAttitude for Day #564: *Blessed are those who help others to learn, for they shall bask in the glow of knowledge shared.*

Fran Stewart

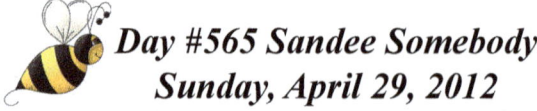
Day #565 Sandee Somebody
Sunday, April 29, 2012

How frustrating! I know that many people put in spam filters that allow messages only from specific eddresses, but I don't give out my personal eddress to the whole world. Instead I use an eddress that is related to my work as an author.

Yesterday a fan I've never met before, Sandee no-last-name, sent me an ecstatic email about how much she enjoyed my Biscuit McKee series, particularly the cat Marmalade. I wrote her an extensive reply, sent it from my personal email, since that's the only way my computer will send anything, only to have it bounce back. I'm sure she probably put fran at you-know-what into her safe list. There was, unfortunately, no form where I could say – hey! please recognize me, I'm your new author friend.

So, I'm going to share her email to me and my reply to her (obviously, I'll block out her eddress and my own). If you think you know her, please send her a link to this blog post, would you?

Here's her email to me:

> On Apr 27, 2012, at 8:22 PM, _____ wrote:
> Subject: Marmy's Series!
> I know, I know it's not Marmalade's series but I like her better! My question is, when are you coming out with more books in the series?
>
> I need for you to write faster if you don't mind! I dearly love this series and have managed, since discovering it just a few short weeks ago, to devour it at a rate of speed I haven't reached since my teens. So now I am suffering from Marmy withdrawals.
>
> Seriously...when are the next books coming out?
>
> I thank you for writing a series that is very enduring and entertaining with enough mystery to keep your interest without sex, graphic

violence, and vulgarity. Thank you!
NOW WRITE FASTER! LOL

Blessings from one of your oldest (in years) fans,
Sandee

And here was my reply to her:

Date: April 28, 2012 7:55:07 AM EDT
To: _____

Sandee, you just brightened my day. Thank you so much for having taken the time to contact me. It's such a delight to hear from people who love Marmy as much as I do. And—I must agree—she's the glue that holds the series together.

As to when Brown as Fudge will be available? I don't have a clue. It will most likely be next year. And there's a good reason for this. The crime in BROWN involves arson. I don't know enough about fire to be able to write knowledgeably about it, so I joined the Gwinnett County Citizen Fire Academy, a twelve-week course that teaches citizens about fire, firefighters, the firefighting process, swift-water rescue, ladder and hose work, and arson investigation.

Unfortunately, after only five classes, I had to drop out (last week) because I'm dealing with a rectal prolapse (which may be more information than you want to have – sorry!). Because of some commitments over the next month and a half, both mine and my daughter's (she's agreed to care for me the first week after the operation), it will be after the 19th of June before I can get this repaired. In the meantime, there's no way I can climb those fire ladders next week or crawl through the "burning" building (fake smoke, naturally) the week after that.

Once I'm done healing, I'll be able to take the NEXT class, which begins in August.

Fran Stewart

So, BROWN is on hold for the moment. I'm writing the non-fire scenes, but the story hasn't taken much shape yet.

You might be interested to know that I was contacted by a New York agent last month and asked if I'd be interested in writing a three-book series "with a Scottish flavor." I've put a proposal together, and the agent will be presenting it to a publisher this coming week. The series won't have a cat in it, but I hope you'll consider reading it when it finally does get published. Of course, the publishing industry has its own routine, so the first Peggy Winn ScotShop mystery may not show up for another year or so (and it may not even be called that by the time their editor gets finished with me).

As a special thank you to you - here's the very first scene of BROWN AS FUDGE. It could change completely before publication, but I'd like to give you the flavor of it:

Scene 1 Biscuit

I saw the smoke even before I stepped outside. A dark gray wash, almost black, swirled across the yard, pushed by a stronger-than-usual early morning breeze. It wasn't leaf-burning season yet. I headed back inside for the phone.

"Thank you for calling," the 911 Operator told me, "but we've already received several reports, and the Martinsville fire department is on the scene."

She wouldn't tell me where the scene was, though. "Stay where you are, ma'am. They don't need unnecessary bystanders getting in the way."

Unnecessary bystanders? What made her think I was unnecessary? I picked the receiver back up. Bob was at the station. He'd know what was going on.

Softfoot is near the fire. I can feel him inside my head.

Marmalade purred her loud rumble and rubbed against my ankle. She's so soft.

Thank you.

Reebok answered on the first ring. "Martinsville Police. Deputy Garner speaking."

"What's going on Reebok? I called 911, but they wouldn't tell me anything."

"There was a fire."

"Where?"

"On Willow Street."

"It wasn't Margaret's house, was it?"

"No." Bob's normally garrulous deputy was singularly taciturn this morning. I waited for him to go on, but there was an ominous silence.

"Monica's?" I asked.

"No."

I was in no mood to keep guessing all the people who lived on Willow. "Whose house?"

"Nobody's house."

"Reebok," I said, my voice lower than usual, "would you please give me some details?"

"The shed behind Connie's house caught fire."

"Is Connie okay?"

Silence.

"Reebok? Answer me."

"Don't worry ma'am, I'm sure it will be all right."

"Reebok? What on earth is wrong?"

"They can't find her."

Have a lovely day,
    --Fran

I really don't want Sandee to think I'm too stuck up to respond to a fan letter. Any idea (other than the miracle of someone who reads this blog knowing her) how I can reach her?

BeeAttitude for Day #565: *Blessed are those who use no pesticides, for they shall create a haven for us bees.*

[2019 Note: Just to give you an idea of how much a book can change through the writing process, not only did the name change to GRAY AS ASHES, but the fire that burned down Connie's shed (her glass-blowing studio), doesn't even occur until the middle of the book. The actual opening paragraph says:

> The second one to burn was my garden shed, and nobody saw anything. Nobody, that is, but the creep who started the fire.

Big difference, eh?

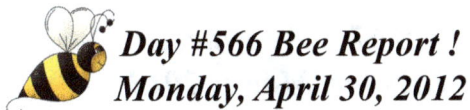

Day #566 Bee Report !
Monday, April 30, 2012

I just heard from Rob Alexander, the man who is caring for my bees. He said he plans to start drawing honey around the first of June. So – you and I have something to look forward to:

- I get to figure out how to handle fresh honey, and
- You get to read about it!

Hope that surgery schedule doesn't interfere with my honey collection ...

I guess my bees are doing pretty well, which is good to know. I was looking out at the back deck yesterday – actually, I look out there every day – and stood there wondering how my bees are getting through this wonderful nectar season.

Then, just as I was getting misty-eyed, a sweet little honeybee flew past the window, right at my eye level, and I felt darn good.

I know all the bees that were here in my hives and then were moved elsewhere have lived through their life-cycle, but I'd like to hope that a little bit of Harbour House lives on in their descendants – the ones who are making the honey that will end up back here at Harbour House.

BeeAttitude for Day #566: *Blessed are those who truly care for us honeybees, for we shall surprise them occasionally with a flyby when it's least expected.*

Day #567 Baby Bluebirds !
Tuesday, May 1, 2012

About all you can see in this picture is four bulgy dark blue tightly closed eyes. My granddaughter Savannah and I took a peek Monday afternoon while Mama Bluebird perched on the phone line overhead and eyed us suspiciously.

This year, I hope I'll finally get to see the babies when they fly for the first time. I've never yet seen the bluebirds take off, although I did see the Carolina wren babies when they fledged a couple of years ago, and my heart still feels all warm thinking about that sight.

BeeAttitude for Day #567: *Blessed are those who make nesting places available (for us bees as well as for those birds), for they shall have buzzing and songs to brighten their days.*

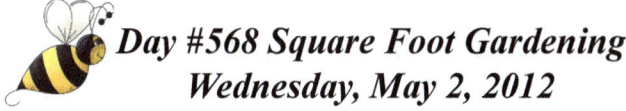 Day #568 Square Foot Gardening
Wednesday, May 2, 2012

Amazing what you can find on the Internet. And amazing how many people can find you.

Yesterday I received an email from someone named Christine, who said she'd discovered my blog while doing research on square foot gardening. Remember I told you on Day #559 about the raised garden kit I'd bought at Home Depot?

Well, she thought I might be interested in the FrugalDad site, where there are instructions on how to build a "square-foot" garden (actually four-feet square - the same size as the kit I bought) for under $50. [**2019 note**: the link she gave me no longer works]

If you build one, send me a picture of it, and I'll post it here on BeesKnees. For that matter, send me a picture of any ole garden you happen to have. Maybe it'll inspire me to finish mine.

BeeAttitude for Day #568: *Blessed are those who raise vegetables for us bees to pollinate, for they shall have good food and our music, too.*

Happy Birthday, Veronica!
I'm so glad you were born!

Fran Stewart

Day #569 Houses for Other Kinds of Bees
Thursday, May 3, 2012

My dear friend Ellen Norton told me she'd installed some houses for native Mason Bees in her Arizona yard, and even sent me the instructions for how to build one. She got information about the bees from the folks at The Pollen Path LLC (note the copyright info beneath. If you choose to share it, please give credit where credit is due).

Incidentally, did you know that the Pollen Path is a Navajo term and relates to the life-giving properties of pollen?

I like to encourage any process that will help bees, whether honeybees or the native pollinators that like to live in these little works of art.

Here's Ellen's bee box:

And here's the information from The Pollen Path. [**2019 Note:** I couldn't find this info anywhere, so I'm now not sure just which website it came from, but I found a current one that I'll show you below this post.]
= = = = = = = = = =
"Pollen Bee Habitat" © 06/1997

Solitary Native Bees: These friendly, solitary non-aggressive creatures will lay 4-8 eggs per hole. They will then line the hole with bee bread made of pollen and nectar for their young. The hole will then be packed with mud or plant cuttings. Your bees will emerge in early spring.

Place your house as a nest or as garden ornamentation among your flowers in early spring, 2 to 3 feet off the ground facing the south or east sun.

These little bees will keep you and your gardens happy and tranquil all summer long.

Note: When you notice an opening in the seal of mud or plant cuttings, clean out the hole making way for future occupants.
==========

2019 Note: Here's the newer (May, 2019) and in my opinion more helpful article:
https://lifehacker.com/how-to-correctly-set-up-a-mason-bee-house-1834551902

BeeAttitude for Day #569: *Blessed are those who sing as they work, for they shall be endlessly entertained.*

Fran Stewart

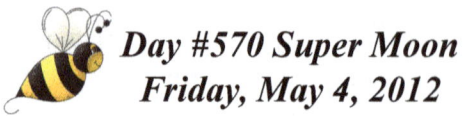

Day #570 Super Moon
Friday, May 4, 2012

From sunset until 11:53 pm tomorrow, May 5th, you'll have a chance to see a Super Moon. Put it on your calendar right now so you'll remember.

Here's a picture from the Nasa.gov site of the Super Moon of March 2011 rising over Lincoln Center:

Super Moons occur when the moon is closest to the earth on the night of a full moon. This makes it appear a whole lot bigger and a whole lot brighter than usual. This happens seldom enough to make it a big event when it does.

If you get a good picture of the moon tomorrow night, send me a copy, and I'll post it here on the blog.

BeeAttitude for Day #570: *Blessed are those who go out at night and look up. We bees don't do that, but we've heard that people see wonders untold.*

Day #571 Miss Polly and Rabindranath Tagore
Saturday, May 5, 2012

I've been thinking about death lately—not from any sort of morbid ponderings, but simply as a way of dealing with the fact that Miss Polly (my alarm cat—see Day #385) will be 16 in five more days. When she came to me as a little rescue kitten, I couldn't believe we'd have this long an association or that she'd become as much of a treasure to me as she is.

I honestly don't know what I'm going to do when it's time for her to go.

The first time a cat of mine died, there were ten others to ease my grief. Gradually, over the years, the numbers have dwindled, and now there are only two. It feels a bit like Agatha Christie's amazing mystery *And Then There Were None*.

Just when I was beginning to get a bit depressed, though, I came across a quotation from Rabindranath Tagore (the one who wrote, "God respects me when I work, but God loves me when I sing") that I'd written on a stray piece of paper – there are a lot of those in my house:

> "Nirvana is not the blowing out of the candle.
> It is the extinguishing of the flame because day is come."
> --Rabindranath Tagore

I'm going to see a candle every time I look at Miss Polly from now on—for as long as I have with her until she passes into her special day.

p.s. Remember to look for the Super Moon tonight!

BeeAttitude for Day #571: *Blessed are those who appreciate the bees around them, for they shall feel a part of something bigger than themselves.*

Fran Stewart

Day #572 Bare Feet and Wet Slides
Sunday, May 6, 2012

Yesterday I spent the day at the Harris Arts Center in Calhoun GA, signing books in the morning and conducting a writer's workshop in the afternoon. One of the benefits of the workshop was that the attendees would get not only a copy of my writer's workbook, but also handouts with writing exercises and additional "stuff" to think about—stuff that will hopefully help them to improve their writing.

One of the handouts was a copy of an essay I wrote for publication in July of 2010. It's kind of fun, and I think you'll be able to enjoy it even if you're not a writer. Here it is:

Bare Feet and Wet Slides - Misplaced Modifiers

Last month I saw a lovely example of misplaced modifiers on my way to the AWC annual picnic. I love signs that are placed strategically halfway up a steep hill. They give me the perfect excuse to pause ostensibly to read them while in reality I am merely catching my breath.

I read somewhere or other of studies having been conducted in playgrounds, comparing an empty city lot, strewn with broken glass, rusty metal, and discarded splinter-ridden wood, to a scientifically-designed, primary-colored, splinter-free wonderland. Guess where the most injuries occurred? Uh-huh. In the "safe" place. Which may be why rules and warning signs are posted in the so-called safe play areas.

At any rate, the ten or twelve RULES were clearly delineated. I admit I didn't read them all. I got stuck on number three. *Do Not*, it said—and the excessive capital letters were theirs, not mine—*Use Equipment When Wet*. Hmm. When the equipment is wet? Or when I am wet? Regardless of what the intent of the rule was, why ever not? Slides are great fun when they're wet. And if I'm the one who's wet, what's the difference?

In our litigious-minded society, such CYA signs are as ubiquitous as they are silly. It seems to me that I should be responsible for my own safety or for that of my children. Common sense and a few basic precepts of cause and effect truly ought to prevent most mishaps. Rather like judicious editing, which ought to prevent the publication of hogwash.

I made it to rule number five before I gave up. *Bare Feet May Cause Injury*. Hmm, again. I suppose any sort of foot might conceivably cause injury, whether or not it is bare, but only if that foot is used, inadvertently or intentionally, as a weapon. The fact that I can surmise what the rule-writer intended to say is not the point. The point is that our sloppy rule-writer did not say what he or she intended. First of all, rule number five is not really a rule; it's a badly phrased warning. *Bare feet may result in injury* would make more sense, although trying to keep children from running around barefoot on the off-hand chance that an injury might occur makes about as much sense as keeping wet people off the slides, or keeping people off the wet slides. At a retreat several years ago, I walked through glowing coals, hot enough to melt a car engine, and still have my feet intact. Bare feet may, therefore, not necessarily result in injury.

While we're talking about the effective use of the English language – we are talking about that in one form or another – I should mention that when I was in seventh grade I was the star ghost-story raconteur at every sleepover my friends and I had. I was, that is, until the fateful night I ruined a perfectly good story by describing a ghost who was inching its way up a staircase, making a clutching sound. Giggles erupted as eight little girls tried to figure out what a clutching sound would sound like. "The ghost's hands made noise as they clutched the banister," I tried to explain, but it was too late. The mood was destroyed and I never did get to finish the story. Every time I got to the staircase, hilarity ensued.

So, maybe I'm overly sensitive about misplaced modifiers, but I do strongly object to the sloppy use of the English language. Rules that make no sense. Warnings that are just plain silly. Stories that never make it to the ghostly ending.
* * *

Just for the fun of it – tell somebody a good story today, preferably without clutching sounds.

BeeAttitude for Day #572: *Blessed are those who walk outside each day, for they shall—perhaps—see us bees and bee gladdened by the sight.*

Day #573 Moon Photos and Chicken Eggs
Monday, May 7, 2012

My friend Ellen Norton, who lives in Arizona, sent me this picture of the Super Moon last Saturday night.

Keep in mind that Ellen is not a professional photographer. Nor is she a professional astronomer. She was simply someone who read about the Super Moon in my blog last week and decided not only to try to see it, but to reply to my challenge to photograph it.

Do you have any idea how good that makes me feel?

Although I started this blog simply as a way to spread information about honeybees and as a way to share with you my excitement about them, the blog has evolved, through many phases. I learned about bees; I planned for their arrival; I picked them up and installed them on my deck; I worked with them (and THOSE were days of a lot of ups and downs). But, most of all, I enjoyed them. I gloried in their sweet presence in my life.

You also shared my anguish when I developed an allergy to their stings, as I contemplated what I was going to do, how I was going to handle this new development. You saw them leave, and I'm sure you heard my cry, even though it was a written one.

Fran Stewart

Now I still talk about bees (sometimes), but I've found many other adventures to share with you. And sometimes, you've taken me up on those adventures, even though I've been unable to join in myself. For example: the Super Moon Saturday night. Calhoun GA was cloudy. Tempe AZ wasn't. Thank you, Ellen.

Example number 2:
When I wrote about getting over my fear of chickens on Day #293, it inspired one of my blog-readers, Geri Taran, to install chickens in her back yard.
- Esmerelda is an Americauna
- Tootsie is a Whiterock
- Roxie is a Barred Rock
- Isabella is a New Hampshire Red, and
- Negrita is a Black Copper Marans.

Now, I occasionally buy eggs from Geri, and I know they came not only from chickens I've met, but from chickens I know by name.

Moon photos and chicken eggs. Those, my friends, are only two of the many wonderful benefits to having kept a blog for all these days.

BeeAttitude for Day #573: *Blessed are those who explore new fields of flowers, for they shall find nectar and pollen they never knew existed.*

Day #574 Aurora Borealis from the ISS
Tuesday, May 8, 2012

Speaking of the moon, as we were yesterday, here's a story from NASA: time-lapse photography of the earth taken by the astronaut crew of the International Space Station's Expedition 30: http://www.youtube.com/watch?v=hWz5ltE_I4c&feature=player_embedded

Here's the run-down of what's happening at which point in the video:
0:01 -- Stars over southern United States
0:08 -- US west coast to Canada
0:21 -- Central Europe to the Middle East
0:36 -- Aurora Australis over the Indian Ocean
0:54 -- Storms over Africa
1:08 -- Central United States
1:20 -- Midwest United States
1:33 -- United Kingdom to Baltic Sea
1:46 -- Moonset 1:55 -- Northern United States to Eastern Canada
2:12 -- Aurora Australis over the Indian Ocean
2:32 -- Comet Lovejoy
2:53 -- Aurora Borealis over Hudson Bay
3:06 -- United Kingdom to Central Europe

The green aurora borealis and aurora australis you'll see in this video are precisely like what I saw years ago from the back deck of our house in Vermont. Seeing those green swirling, waving curtains above me was an awesome experience that's almost impossible to describe. Now you get a chance to share it. Around the world in four minutes.

I'm glad that my friend Judi A. Winall, an incredible photographer whose Master's thesis I supervised, took the time to send the link to me.

BeeAttitude for Day #574: *Blessed are those who travel far and blessed are those who don't, for they shall all see wonder if their eyes and their hearts are open.*

Day #575 Taking a Sabbatical for a Month or So
Wednesday, May 9, 2012

I know that when I made the commitment to blog every day for 600 days, I felt bound and determined to keep to that promise. And so far, I haven't missed a single day.

Life has gotten in the way, though. Two weeks from today I'll be in surgery, looking at a month-long recovery period afterwards. The cow here seems to be saying, "And here's what I think about that!"

Do you remember how, when I went to Disney World a few months back, I wrote and scheduled my blog posts ahead of time (without telling you until afterwards) so that in case I couldn't get Internet access, I wouldn't miss any blog days? Then, when I came home, I posted pictures and shared stories from that trip.

I did that primarily because I make it a point never to put anything on the Internet that says, "Oh, by the way, my house will be standing untended for a week or more. Please come rob away."

This time, that stricture doesn't apply, since I have house sitters and cat sitters and bird-feeder fillers and yard carers lined up by the ying-yang. My cats and birds and flowers will be perfectly content while I heal.

I've taken a good look at my energy level, which has been decreasing a little bit each day for the last couple of months. So, I've decided to take care of myself. I won't be spending the energy it takes to post something every single day. In fact, I'm taking a sabbatical for a whole month. As much as I enjoy writing these posts, the blogging process has become a chore—something I have to find the energy for and then make myself do—and I don't ever want to approach my beloved writing that way. The blog isn't the only thing I'm putting on hold. I'm not taking on any more editing clients for now.

Flowers and trees conserve their energy during the winter, pulling back as necessary. Bees cluster in the hive in the winter, keeping themselves warm enough for survival. I feel like this is what I'm doing. Withdrawing into my hive to gather strength for the coming endeavor. I plan to come back from this surgery not only healed, but thriving indeed.

I would appreciate any good thoughts you can send my way, both as I approach the surgery-day and as I recover afterwards.

I'll be back with post #576 sometime in mid-to-late June, and I WILL finish the 600 days. Thank you for sticking with me.

p.s. Feel free to email me or message me through Facebook/FranStewartAuthor. I love hearing from you, although I might not be able to respond for a while.

BeeAttitude for Day #575: *Blessed are those who fly to the fields they can reach, leaving enough energy to get back home, for they shall find new stores of energy when it's time to fly again.*

Day #576 So It Was More Than 3 Months
Monday, August 20, 2012

I know I said I'd be gone for a month or so, and that was three months and 11 days ago. Sorry about that.

It's been a busy three months – the first one was spent learning how to ask for help – not something I was real good at. A rectocele repair turned out to be a lot more major than I had thought it was going to be. Dr. Hearrin said it was a very common surgery. When I told him I'd never heard of it before, he said, "How many people do you know who are willing to talk about their rectum in public?"

I guess he had a point.

Well, I'm here to say the surgery was successful; once the stitches were out, I started getting right back to normal. Don't pay attention to all the horror stories you read on the Internet. As with any surgery, things can go wrong, but usually they don't.

In July, as a reward to myself for healing so well, I went with a group of artists to Sapelo Island for a five-day retreat. What an absolutely magical time that was. This was during the time that Venus, Jupiter, and the Moon were putting on quite a display, so 4 or 5 of us got up at 5:00 each morning, drove a mile to Nanny Goat Beach in a quiet little golf cart, and watched the wonder. Then we watched the dawn, which was pretty wonderful as well. My photos can't possibly do justice to it, but I'm including a couple to give you an idea.

While I was there, I tried to call my e-friend (and frequent blog-commenter) Petie Ogg, on her birthday, but there's no cellphone service on the eastern side of the island.

Ah well, I DID think about you, Petie. Hope you and your twin had a great day. Happy (Late) Birthday!

Tomorrow I'll tell you a few more details about the surgery, in case you're interested. You may know someone who's facing the same sort of problem. Of course, they may not have shared with you that they're facing it. After all, who (except Fran) talks about that in public?

It's good to be back!

BeeAttitude for Day #576: *Blessed are those who love the work they do, for they shall have a full basket of joy each day.*

Fran Stewart

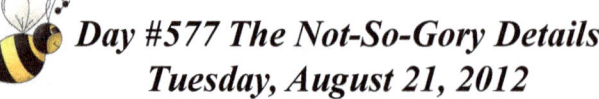 ***Day #577 The Not-So-Gory Details***
Tuesday, August 21, 2012

About three weeks after the rectocele repair surgery, I emailed Petie about the experience. I'm sharing part of that email with you. If you don't read anything else, read the second paragraph of the email:

= = = = = = = = = =

As to the surgery? Well, dear friend, it could have been a lot worse. I went on line yesterday and found all sorts of horror stories about people who'd had rectocele repair surgery – glad I didn't read any of them beforehand. The surgery was successful, but what I'd thought would be a simple one or two-week recovery period is stretching out much longer. I still can't drive – still can't sit comfortably. I'm STANDING at the kitchen counter right now, with my laptop on it. That's the only way I can handle e-stuff.

I made hospital history by being the only person the nurses had ever seen who'd gone through this type of surgery without any narcotics for pain management. Despite an anesthesiologist who ARGUED with me ("You're going to need it. The pain will be horrible otherwise") and a surgeon who was vocally supportive at my pre-op appointment ("Sure - we can try intravenous Tylenol") but who left the operating room to tell my friends in the waiting room that, although the surgery had been successful, "She's going to need morphine to handle the pain. I know she wants to do it without narcotics, but be sure you encourage her to ask for the morphine when she needs it." Good grief. Not only did I not need it, I wasn't even tempted. The Tylenol worked just fine. On a scale of 1 to 10, my pain was zero. Of course, when I left the hospital the next day, things became a bit more challenging—okay, quite a bit more—but I'm dealing with them. Without narcotics.

My blessed friends in the area have been so supportive. Don't know how hermits manage. Scooping litter boxes, bringing food, returning library books, checking my P.O. box, driving me to the doc for my two-week follow-up appointment. I tend to forget how much I use my car, until I can't drive any more. It'll be another two weeks, probably...

I was feeling like a real wimp there for a while, but I ended up calling the surgeon's office a week and a half after the surgery. Talked to the nurse. "I run out of breath and run out of energy all the time," I whined, "and the stitches itch and I can't sit down without crying." I might have gone on like that a long time, but when I paused to take a breath she said, "Sweetie, you've had major surgery. Your body needs all that energy that you usually spend on other activities just to heal." She went on to say that this type of surgery is worse for women than a hysterectomy. Just have to give myself time to heal.

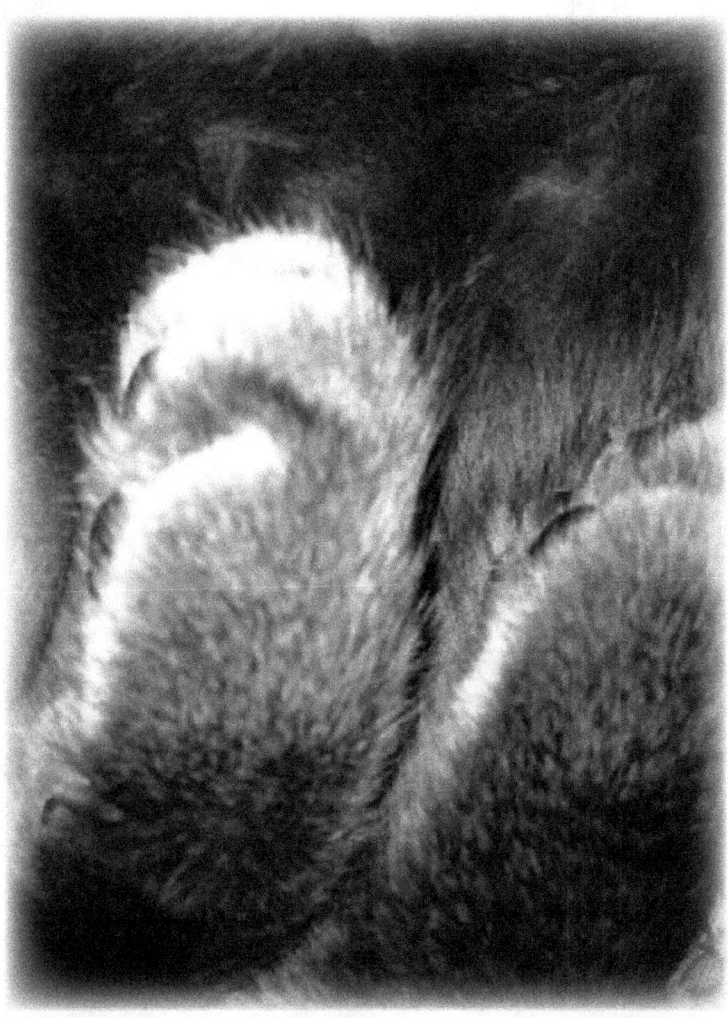

So, that explains the four naps a day. Miss Polly absolutely loves it, because she gets to curl up in the curve of my body and keep my tummy warm. The other day I woke up to find her in the crook of my arm. I managed to take a picture of her paws and this one of her face before she squirmed out of range.

There is something so comforting about my old green flannel shirt when I'm feeling lousy. Add a cat, and the picture is perfect.

Then I noticed that Daisy was asleep on the piano. She stayed there until I could get up. Photo's fuzzy, but I love the way it shows her perky white whiskers:

And this daylily (first one to bloom this summer) was waiting for me when I finally made it to the mailbox.

Enough. Time for my second nap of the day.
   --Fran
==========

A week later, I was begging a friend to bring me M&Ms - I was VERY tired of eating all the healthy stuff. And she did! Thank you, Mikki!

BeeAttitude for Day #577: *Blessed are those who bring whatever is needed when asked to do so, for they shall create happiness.*

Fran Stewart

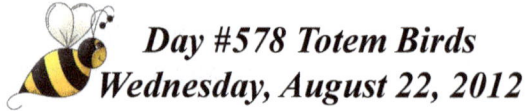

Day #578 Totem Birds
Wednesday, August 22, 2012

Every once in a while, something happens that is so out-of-the-ordinary I simply have to share it. I hope you haven't gotten tired about my (two so far) surgery stories, because I have one more for you:

Around about the time I was beginning to circle the wagons, not able to go anywhere or do anything, a friend of mine told me, "There are going to be so many angels around you, you'll probably be able to smell the feathers!"

We laughed, and I didn't think much more about it.

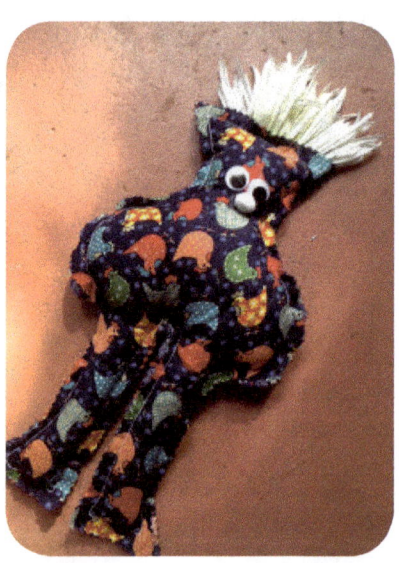

On the morning of the surgery, David Hamilton showed up at the hospital at 6 a.m. to be with me and give me Reiki throughout the surgery. He brought with him a little chicken-fabric doll he'd made himself. It was infused with Reiki energy. Sticking out from the top of its crazy little head was a row of (fake) feathers. Ha. Ha. Isn't that a funny coincidence? Smell-the-feathers jokes. He said it was called a Dammit Doll—get angry or upset about something, and all you have to do is slam the dammit doll against the nearest hard object.

Although the hospital wouldn't allow David in the operating room, they did let me have the chicken in there. The chicken was on my tummy when I woke up in the recovery room to see David there, pouring Reiki energy into me. His sweet being helped calm me from the effects of the anesthesia.

When they took me to my room, they asked David to leave for a few minutes so they could get me settled. He walked out to the end of the hallway, where a big window overlooked the rooftop of another hospital wing. As he stood there, two vultures descended and spread their wings. He took this picture through the thick plate glass of the window. Even through the distortion of the window, their wings and their shadows show clearly.

Now, the funny thing about vultures is that they are unique in the bird kingdom. Their digestive systems are capable of destroying the plague virus, and any other yucky stuff that might go through. You're welcome to disagree, but I'm pretty sure those two came to say that I would be safe – that no disease would get through into me.

They also pee on their own feet, which helps kill germs as well, but I'm not gonna go there.

BeeAttitude for Day #578: *Blessed are those who see how pollen and nectar lead to honey, for they shall appreciate us bees.*

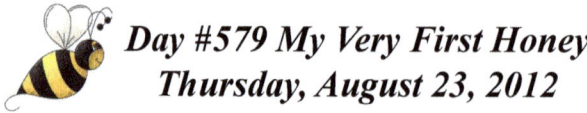 Day #579 My Very First Honey
Thursday, August 23, 2012

Honey! Honey! I have honey!

You'd think, from those exclamation points that I harvested some today, but the truth is that I've had it for about a month. And I'm still excited about it.

The hives that I donated to Rancho Alegre made it through the winter, but Rob said only one of them was producing enough to harvest. He gave me half the honey (since I gave him the use of the bee hives), and I ended up with TWO GALLONS.

It's been so much fun, having honey to give as gifts. And fun, too, to watch the faces of my grandchildren as they discover real honey (as opposed to store-bought, part high-fructose corn syrup honey). This stuff is just plain ole downright delicious!

Because Rob harvested the honey in June, and I still wasn't supposed to lift anything much heavier than a quart of milk, my dear friend and fellow beekeeper Geri Taran bottled the honey up for me in jars I'd been collecting for ages.

She even put on some of my stickers that say:

> How do you know
> it's pure honey
> if you don't know
> the beekeeper?

Here's just one of the happy, beautiful jars:

BeeAttitude for Day #579: *Blessed are friends who help when help is needed, for they shall rest easy.*

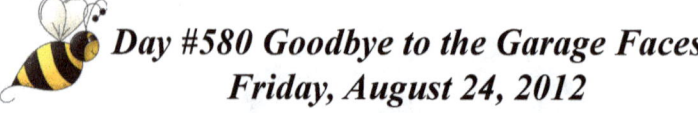 Day #580 Goodbye to the Garage Faces
Friday, August 24, 2012

Remember when I shared with you those cute faces that have lived on my garage doors ever since the summer seven years ago when I moved into this house?

Well, we have to say goodbye to them. I received a notice from the Police Department saying that I had to remove the "graffiti" – I kid you not, that's what they called it – from my garage doors.

So, here's a very sad goodbye to these cute little folk:

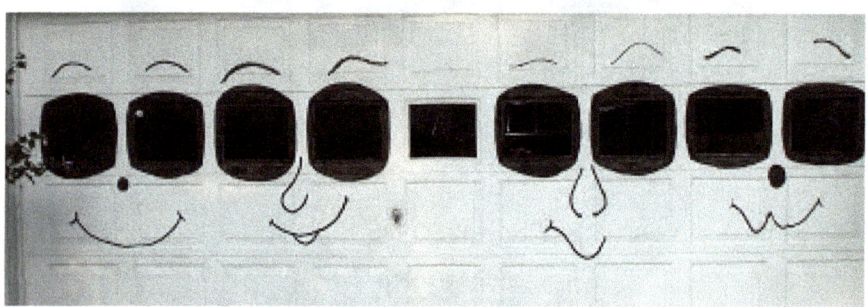

I've just about decided to paint the garage doors either bright purple or emerald green. What would you vote for?

BeeAttitude for Day #580: *Blessed are those who fly with flexibility, for they shall have a much more interesting flight through life.*

Day #581 The World in a Simple Rug
Saturday, August 25, 2012

At the risk of sounding like a pale reflection of something out of *Horton Hears a Who*, I'd like to tell you about a world I found in a section of rug.

This rug has seen better days. It used to be in my daughter's house. When she was getting ready to toss it out (about 15 years ago), I said, "Naw, don't do that. I'll take it off your hands."

What I actually did was take it off the top of her big blue garbage bin.

I hate to see things wasted.

She'd had various dogs, and later, children. I've had various cats. The rug has, as I mentioned, been through a lot and come out—well, I'd say it's come out pretty well considering all it's been through.

For some reason, don't ask me why, I decided to get down on my hands and knees and take a really close look at this entity that has shared my living room, my family room, and now my office for such a long time. I walk across it all day long, but seldom look at it.

Hence the hands-and-knees bit.

As you can see from the above photo, there are quite a few flowers and fanciful leaves on it, each one formed by multiple tiny loops, each loop a specific color. They're getting rather mushed down.

But then, out of lingering curiosity, I turned back a corner of it. The pattern is just as striking on the other side.

The colors are softer somehow. I should think they'd be brighter, since they've never seen the sun, but the greens aren't as green.

Hmm. There probably is some deep philosophical lesson in all this – something about how the different aspects of a person come out in different ways under different circumstances – just how much sun has there been in someone's life?—and so on.

Then again, maybe this is just a rug.

With toes on one edge of it.

There HAS to be a story in that...

BeeAttitude for Day #581: *Blessed are those who let native vines clamber around the yard, for they shall be rewarded by seeing us bees when the flowers bloom.*

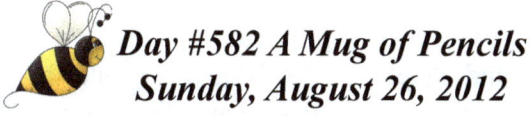

Day #582 A Mug of Pencils
Sunday, August 26, 2012

What is it about a cup full of pens and pencils? I have one in almost every room of my house. Well, okay, you're right. I'm a writer. But I don't need thirty pencils, forty pens, and three big fat erasers for that. One pencil, one notebook (at a time), and one computer keyboard should do it.

Still, I find a certain measure of contentment when I look at those sharpened pencils, propped in an old snowman mug, ready to be picked up and written with. There's so much possibility there.

And, speaking of possibilities, I just have to share something with you. Friday I sent in a proposal for a three-book mystery series to a New York agent who had contacted me some months ago. His first email to me said that he thought I'd be the perfect person to write a series he had in mind. He gave me very few details, just one phrase to pique my curiosity. The books, he said, would have a "Scottish flavor."

Well, knock me over with a bagpipe, I said yes pretty quickly. We've been trading emails and chapter drafts for a while, and the proposal is finally ready. Now it's in his court. He said an editor he'd already talked with was "very interested."

What does that mean? Don't ask me. I haven't a clue how that part of the publishing industry works. All I know is that I'm pretty excited about the nine chapters I've written so far. As time goes on, I'll share more details with you about how this process works.

And you will definitely be invited to the launch party!

p.s. I can't even tell you the name of the series or the proposed names for the three books. Publishing houses often change the names. That's why what we send to an agent is said to have a "working title." That means *don't get attached to it*.

BeeAttitude for Day #582: *Blessed are those who hum along with us bees. It doesn't prove anything, but it brightens the world a bit.*

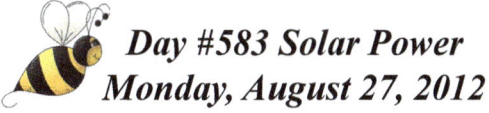 Day #583 Solar Power
Monday, August 27, 2012

Beehives like to be in the full sun, or at least only partial shade. When they're in full shade, it's easier for mites and stuff to grow in the hive and weaken the bees. I'm not sure why, but that's what I've read. Bees are very efficient, as I've mentioned before in this blog, about cooling their hives in the summer and warming themselves in the winter.

Some people are like bees. They need lots of sun, full sun. Those are the folks who migrate (or wish they could) south—or, for my Australian readers, north.

I would have made a lousy honeybee. I'm a shade kind of person. That's one reason I'm real happy with these woods behind my house. And people, unlike bees, don't necessarily have to sicken in the shade. In fact, they can thrive.

In the summer, while my neighbors up the street are enjoying (or not, as the case may be) the western sun through their windows, I'm wallowing in delicious, soft, cool (sort of) shade. At least, it's cooler than up the street.

And my electricity bill last month for this all-electric house was only $37.

Not too shabby, eh?

BeeAttitude for Day #583: *Blessed are those who sing to the sun and the wind, for their wings shall be uplifted with joy.*

 *Day #584 Wish I Could Remember*
Tuesday, August 28, 2012

No, this is not a post about Alzheimer's, although with such a title, one might think so.

Years ago I read one of those quotable quotations, and I know the author was mentioned, but over the years I've simply forgotten who said it or wrote it to begin with.

One day, a woman knelt beside her house.
A man ran up and said, "What would you do if you knew that you would die within the next hour?"
She looked up and smiled. "I'd finish planting this tree."

I thought about this because someone commented about yesterday's post, saying that between hurricanes and tornados, they hadn't a tree left in their yard.

What to do?

My advice would be to plant a forest. A single tree here and there can be bowled over by the wind. As trees are grouped together, though, they seem to provide protection to each other.

My neighbors up the hill have a grove in their whole front yard. The only mowing they ever have to do is around the edges. It's wonderful!

While a single tree spreading over an open field might be a beautiful, even awe-inspiring sight, that tree is highly susceptible to lightning damage. As trees cluster together, though, leaving enough room for roots and canopy, they divide the danger and multiply the benefits.

If you can't plant a forest, at least try for a grove. One or two tall native species trees, intermingled with four or five lower-story trees can create a natural picnic spot (in about twenty years). And some lovely shade well before then.

I have a bunch of Arbor Day trees that I received seven years ago in return for a small donation. I now have yard chairs underneath a couple of them, and the shade is restful indeed.

A single tree is like a single bee.

BeeAttitude for Day #584: *Blessed are those who plant trees that flower, for we bees shall help those trees (and those people) thrive.*

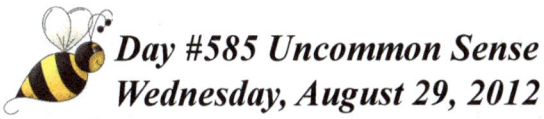 *Day #585 Uncommon Sense*
Wednesday, August 29, 2012

In 1986 I bought a book. I read it and underlined a lot of passages. The book was a series of common sense essays. When I moved from Vermont to Georgia in 1993, I packed the book away in a box.

I did finally unpack it (probably in about 1997 or 98), stuck it on a bookcase, and pretty much forgot about it.

Kim Williams' *Book of Uncommon Sense: A Practical Guide With 10 Rules for Nearly Everything* sat there for a while, got put into another box seven – almost eight – years ago when I moved to this house, and has lived on yet another bookshelf for quite a while.

What on earth must Ms. Williams think of me for ignoring her such a long time? And what a lot I've missed. The book appears to be out-of-print now, which is a real shame.

It's been interesting to review the things I underlined all those years ago:

- In one essay, next to the phrase "eat a turnip," I wrote, "Yuck." Now, why would I write that? To the best of my knowledge, I had never tasted a turnip.
- In another, an essay about the fun and practicality of potluck dinners, she wrote that the best invitation is "I have the spot. You bring the pot" – even if it's for a wedding reception.
- "Eating bean sprouts will not save your soul."
- And – one of my favorites – "I will not fall into the toothpaste trap. I will write down how much money I spend on toothpaste in a year; then I will spend it on something else." – I vote for this one because my teeth have done quite well for years on a "toothcleaner" mixture of salt and baking soda, moistened with hydrogen peroxide.
- Another little gem – talking about a mountain spring that had a frog living in it – "Funny that we never thought to question the right of that frog to live in our drinking water."

I'd like to keep a little uncommon sense in my life. If I'm missing any, I'd like Ms. Williams to help me usher it back in.

Just wish she were around to bring me a turnip.

BeeAttitude for Day #585: *Blessed are those who provide water for us bees in the summertime, for they shall have the joy of watching us drink and flap our little wings.*

Day #586 Structural Integrated Therapy® Thursday, August 30, 2012

Bees probably don't have back problems. Or if they do, we have no way to find out about it.

But people do. When I was in my 40th year, my mother tried to kill me. It was completely unconscious—at least I hope it was—but she was angry at me for something or other, and she turned her car left into the path of an oncoming vehicle and stopped in the middle of the lane.

The passenger door caved in on me.

The funny thing was that it was November in Colorado, and I was wearing a heavy pair of corduroy slacks. A week or so later, back home in Vermont, I looked down at the side of my leg to find blue, purple, yellow, and green-striped bruises in an exact imprint of the corduroy's wale.

I went to an orthopedist who found that my spine took a rather strange L-shaped bend in the middle, where the top half of the vertebral column was pushed to the left. It's truly a wonder my spinal cord wasn't severed.

A couple of years of pain later, I found a chiropractor and, later still, a neuromuscular massage therapist. Between the two of them, they managed to get my spine back into shape. Thank goodness.

Now I've found someone (something) else. And I have to tell another story to lead into this. When I was in my early thirties I became very, very ill. In the middle of one coughing, vomiting bout, I felt something tear inside me. I asked my then-husband to take me to the emergency room, but there was a flu epidemic going around Vermont at the time. He said—and I'm sure he felt this was quite reasonable—"No. They'll just tell you it's the flu and send you home. You probably pulled a muscle." He went back to the TV and I kept throwing up.

Ten days later I took our two small children to a babysitter, told them

Mommy has to go to the doctor, but I'll be back. I then drove myself to our family doc, who diagnosed a ruptured appendix and told me to have my husband drive me to the emergency room. "I can't," I said. "He's at work."

The doc thought I was crazy. "How did you get here?"

"I drove."

I then drove myself to the hospital, passed out from the pain in the emergency room, and was admitted. They pumped me full of antibiotics overnight and operated the next morning. The after-effects of peritonitis kept me in the hospital for 21 days.

And my kids both developed abandonment issues—I'm sure they must have.

It was a couple of years before I could even touch my abdomen. Although the pain has lessened since then, it's never really gone away.

Now—and this is the point of all this rambling—I've discovered Pam Reagin, who practices Structural Energetic Therapy® in Hoschton, GA. She explained to me that both of these incidents resulted in internal scar tissue, called adhesions. The ones in my neck and spine have pulled one shoulder lower than the other. The ones from the appendectomy have affected my entire belly area.

I've had five or six sessions with Pam now. And I can finally touch my belly—push on it even—with no pain for the first time in more than 30 years. Now she's beginning to work on my neck and collarbone area. I'm looking forward to not being lopsided.

I don't know what sort of adhesions you have—but you might want to Google Structural Energetic Therapy and find someone in your area. If you're in Georgia, email me and I'll give you Pam's number.

Balance is a good thing.

BeeAttitude for Day #586: *Blessed are those who fly carefully, for their wings shall uplift them.*

[**2019 Note:** Forgive the repetition, please. I wrote about the car wreck back on Day #501, and then had forgotten about having done so. You may have found a fair amount of repetition throughout these posts. Think of it in this vein: I like rereading books. So why wouldn't I occasionally repeat myself when I write?]

Fran Stewart

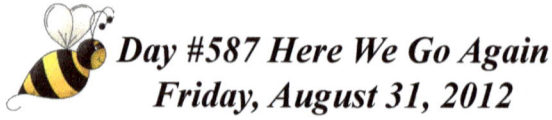 Day #587 Here We Go Again
Friday, August 31, 2012

Remember last April when I had to stop attending the Gwinnett Citizen Fire Academy?

I'd made it all the way through the hose work in the fifth class (see Day #556), but was in too much pain to go any further in the training.

Well, I'm back in class again—this time it's the 18th GCFA. I'm not going to bore you with a repetition of all the stuff we're learning for the next five weeks. After all, I already told you all that stuff in March and April.

I was just getting ready to say that I'll be happy to tell you all about classes 6 through 12 – but it occurred to me that I'll be past my 600 days well before those classes happen.

What to do?

I'm going to think about it.

Should I change this to a once-a-week blog posting?

No. Here's a better idea. I'll figure out a way to do some other blog. Maybe. After all, with the bee allergy, I'm really not interacting with bees much anymore, and these blog entries have ranged far afield of beekeeping.

I know, I know. I can hear you saying—they've ALWAYS ranged far afield. Yeah. You're right.

So, I guess I'll just have to wait for Day #600 to let you know what's going to happen.

With maybe a preview a little before then.

BeeAttitude for Day #587: *Blessed are those who know where the best pollen is, for they shall fly home laden with gold.*

[**2019 Note:** I didn't do another blog, but a couple of years ago I did begin posting on my Facebook author page (FranStewartAuthor) every day, Monday through Saturday. In case you're interested, feel free to follow me there. My next project will be to publish those daily musings both as e-books and print books.]

Day #588 Dog Treats
Saturday, September 1, 2012

For several years, I've been buying special gourmet organic dog treats for my grand dogs - and any other good dogs I happen to run across. I used to buy them at Rancho Alegre in Dacula GA, through Gwinnett Locally Grown, an organization I've talked about before here on BeesKnees.

They were made by an outfit called Chateau le Pup. Don't you love that name? The last time I bought treats, I bought three bags. But then, one day, the gourmet dog treats weren't listed in the GLG online catalog.

YIKES! What was I going to do? My granddogs, Belle and Max (see Day #286), kept running up to me excitedly every time I walked in the door of my daughter's house. They'd gotten used to my having a treat for them.

first day of school 2012

Here's a special picture of Belle - taken by my daughter:

Cheyenne (see Day #409), the official greeter at Wild Birds Unlimited of Suwanee also had me trained to bring her treats each time I went there to buy birdseed.

In this Internet world we live in, you'd think I would have gone to my computer and Googled Chateau le Pup. Did I? Not for a whole bunch of dog-treat-drought months. Duh!

Anyway, the point of all this is that I've found Chateau le Pup treats once again. Amanda, from Chateau le Pup, will be at the Snellville Farmers Market this morning. And I'm gonna go.

I'll probably buy four bags. After all, I've met a lot of other nice dogs lately.

BeeAttitude for Day #588: *Blessed are those who keep looking for nectar and pollen, for they shall eventually find the right flowers.*

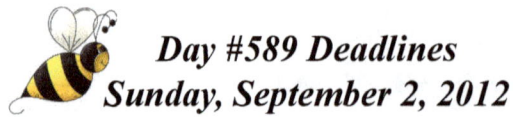

Day #589 Deadlines
Sunday, September 2, 2012

For some reason I've gotten myself into a situation where I'm facing a whole bunch of deadlines.

- Complete the three-book proposal for my agent before tomorrow
- Clean my house (AARGH!) before my sister arrives in two weeks.
- Paint the garage door before October 1st (double-AARGH).
- Find someone who can sharpen the blades to my reel-type mower (or teach me how to do it myself) before … well, soon.
- Complete a rough draft of my newest Biscuit McKee mystery before November 15th.

I know I've brought these on myself. Several of them could have been over and done with already if I'd just DO something (like start the vacuum cleaner).

I'll get number 1 done as soon as I stop typing this blog post. But the rest of them? Guess I can put them off a little while longer.

Self discipline. This week it just ain't happening around this house.

I'm going to go make myself a Blue Bell Ice Cream milkshake.

BeeAttitude for Day #589: *Blessed are those who work as diligently as bees. Blessed are those, also, who flutter as diligently as butterflies, for both shall be content.*

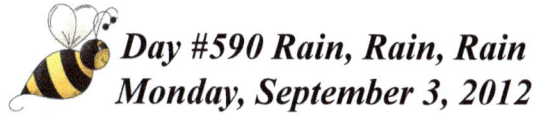 *Day #590 Rain, Rain, Rain*
Monday, September 3, 2012

The ground around here has been gasping for such a long time, but today, there's rain. Not just a little bit. A lot. And it reminds me of something.

I went without a piano for a number of years, from the time I left home to go to college until well into my married life. Finally, though, I got tired of feeling like parched earth. I wanted the rain of music back in my life.

So I bought a piano. The music started falling, just like tentative raindrops. I hadn't touched a piano in so many years, it was almost like starting over again. Scales. Finger-limbering exercises.

But then the floodgates opened, and music filled my life once more.

Nowadays I don't play the piano often. But I sing with the Gwinnett Choral Guild. I play my mini bongo drums just for the fun of it when I walk past the kitchen counter. I hum along as I drive.

It's just like the rain. A little here, a lot there. A little here. Some more there. And my world is satisfied.

BeeAttitude for Day #590: *Blessed are those who fill their combs with pollen and honey, for they shall be well nourished all their life long.*

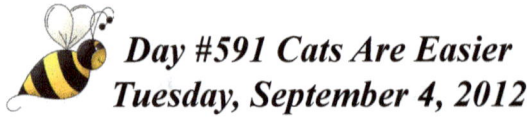 Day #591 Cats Are Easier
Tuesday, September 4, 2012

I've been dog-sitting my granddogs for the past few days.

Whenever my daughter & Edwin have to be out of town, I go over there around 6:30 or 7:00 in the morning and again in the evening to let the dogs out, feed them, play with them a bit. I enjoy doing it.

I've found something interesting. My granddogs seem to be regular muses for me. Whenever I go there, I always stay for an hour or two, and I generally take along some writing or reading to do between play-times.

Saturday morning, I took my computer, because I'd made a lot of corrections/changes to the printed copy of my most recent book endeavor, and I had to get those transferred into cyberese.

I wrote and wrote and wrote.

Ditto Saturday evening and Sunday morning.

When I went back Sunday evening, I wrote and wrote and wrote. It occurred to me to Google a couple of what I thought were facts, but wasn't 100% sure. Sure enough, I'd made a mistake (several of them), which meant I had to go back through the whole manuscript and correct numerous scenes. I'd had my fourteenth century ghost wearing a kilt, for instance, but I found out kilts weren't used until the 1500s. So I put him in a belted plaid, which is much more fun to describe anyway. I had to change his name for his knife from "dirk" to "dagger." Things like that.

I had great fun. The rain was pouring outside, I'd already taken the dogs out to pee, and all was well.

At midnight-thirty I looked at the clock. Ohmigosh. So rather than drive the three and a half miles home, only to have to turn around in a few hours and come right back, I curled up on their couch and slept all night, surrounded by Max lying on the floor beside me and Belle lying on her soft cushion at the end of the couch. I didn't worry about my cats. They had plenty of food and water, and the litter boxes had been scooped.

Max licked me awake at 8:29 - I NEVER sleep that late when I'm at home ! ! !

So we went through the feeding, peeing, playing routine, and then I wrote until about 2:00, when we all went outside again.

Then I drove home, to find Miss Polly and Daisy perfectly content. They did wonder where I'd been overnight, but they each took a sniff at my pant legs and decided that all was okay. They've met Belle, after all, when she used to come for visits, before big ole Max came along.

My daughter and Edwin are home now, safe and sound. And their dogs are, I'm sure, delighted.

As my title for this blog post says, though, Cats Are Easier.

BeeAttitude for Day #591: *Blessed are those who cover their windows so birds and bees won't try to fly through them, for those people will have happy birds. And happy bees, too!*

Fran Stewart

🐝 *#592 DBF in 90-degree weather*
Wednesday, September 5, 2012

Last Saturday, when I was working the Atlanta Writers Club booth at the Decatur Book Festival, a woman stopped by and asked if she could take my picture. "Sure," I said, and held up an AWC brochure.

Mary Gilmartin, the one taking the picture, had invited me a number of months ago to speak to her writers group. I did, and we had a great discussion. It was good to see her again.

Yesterday, she sent me a link to her blog post about the book festival. The following paragraph was just one of many describing the wonders of that Labor Day weekend event. I was honored to have been a part of it, although I didn't see a single honeybee the entire day... Here's what she wrote:

> I first discovered Fran Stewart when she hosted a one-year project in 2009 on Mystery Matters. Every Friday morning she would interview a mystery writer. As an author herself, Fran has written many

books. The first line of Chapter 1 in her first mystery book "Orange as Marmalade" is one of my favorites: "There had definitely not been a body on the second floor landing when I had run upstairs to the attic earlier in the evening."   -- Mary Gilmartin

Thanks for the plug, Mary!

It was a fun, exhausting event. The fact that the temp hovered around 90 degrees the whole time contributed to the exhausting part. Thank goodness for the tent.

BeeAttitude for Day #592: *Blessed are those who share their knowledge with others, for they shall keep the hive functioning smoothly.*

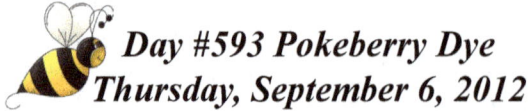 Day #593 Pokeberry Dye
Thursday, September 6, 2012

The next time you eat honey, take a moment to appreciate the work (by the bees) that went into creating it and the work (by humans) that went into harvesting and packaging it. And that reminds me of another close-to-the-land industry: yarn.

When I was in Washington DC a year or so ago, I went to a farmer's market in DuPont Circle and met the wonderful people at Solitude Wool. I signed up for email notices, and I get some of the cutest pictures as a result.

In yesterday's newsletter, they were talking about making dyes from pokeberries. I doubt I could ever gather enough pokeberries because the cardinals in my yard eat them faster than imaginable. At any rate, they gathered a huge pan full of berries, mushed them and strained them, cooked them like crazy for hours and hours, and got enough dye for one skein of yarn.

In their own words, "it took 2.5 pounds of pokeberries to dye 1.6 oz. of yarn. That is nuts! To do a 4-pound dye lot, I would need 100 pounds of pokeberries. Don't expect to be seeing pokeberry dyed yarn for sale at the market..."

BeeAttitude for Day #593: *Blessed are those who appreciate the work we bees do, for their honey shall taste sweeter.*

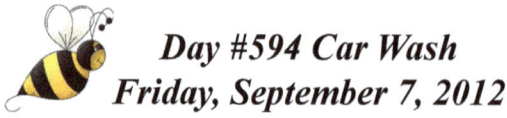 Day #594 Car Wash
Friday, September 7, 2012

I had my car washed a couple of days ago, at no extra charge.

I'd gone to Rancho Alegre, the organic farm in Dacula, GA where I buy produce and meat and all sorts of other goodies.

When I came out, I found that my car had been washed by two of the Rancho Alegre employees.

They did a pretty good job, too. No soap, of course, and the lick marks are hardly distinguishable. Rubbing their sides against the car helped to dry it afterwards.

Of course, I had to wait until the wash and dry was completed before I drove home, but I wasn't in a hurry. I live on bee-time now.

BeesKnees #6: A Beekeeping Memoir

BeeAttitude for Day #594: *Blessed are those who give good value for the jobs they do, for they shall rest easier when they return to the hive.*

Fran Stewart

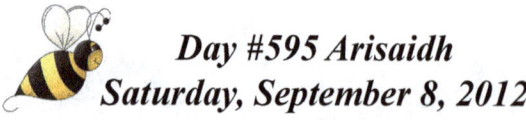

Day #595 Arisaidh
Saturday, September 8, 2012

You'll never guess what I did --

But before I tell you what I did, you'll need to understand that I'm working on a new book - a brand new mystery series that has a character who is from Scotland, and another one with some pretty strong Scottish connections.

I figure I'll be doing some book signings here and there when the book comes out.

So . . .

I bought an arisaidh from Misty Thicket Clothing.

I can hear you. You're saying, "What the heck is an arisaidh?"

I'm glad, as I so often say, that you asked. An arisaidh is sort of a cross between a skirt and a kilt and a cloak, worn by 14th-century women in the Scottish Highlands.

Nowadays the usual spelling is a-r-i-s-a-i-d, but I think it needs that extra letter on the end to make it look - well, Scottish.

It's worn belted around the waist, and the top part can be pinned at the shoulder or used as a cover-up when the weather is inclement – I always wanted an excuse to use that word.

Or it can be worn down.

These pictures are from the Misty Thicket website, by the way.

Keep in mind, I ordered a Stewart Ancient Hunting Tartan (see the example at the top), so the pattern of mine will look different than this one the model is wearing. Mine will have more greens and lighter blues.

And the other difference is that my hair doesn't flow down my back like hers.

<<<<< sigh >>>>>

[**2019 Note:** It's amazing what a few years of growing out your hair can do.]

BeeAttitude for Day #595: *Blessed are those who live life to the fullest, for when their wings wear out, they will be able to say, "Life was good."*

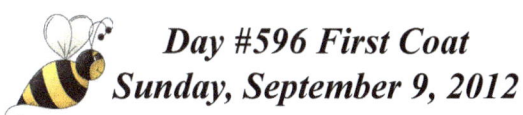 Day #596 First Coat
Sunday, September 9, 2012

The saga continues:

Yesterday morning I got up early, went out and put a first coat of paint on the garage door.

The faces are gone.

Rats!

It still needs a second coat before it looks halfway decent, and I'm almost ashamed to post a picture of it at this stage of the game, but I promised to keep you informed.

Here's the ragged-looking first coat:

Fran Stewart

I'm thinking of putting a thin line of emerald green around the eyes—'scuse me, I mean the windows—to match the shutters. And then I may put a thin line of purple around each emerald green shutter.

We wouldn't want conformity to be too boring, would we?

Several butterflies came by to check it out. The good news is – they didn't land in the wet paint.

I don't think we're in Kansas anymore, Toto.

BeeAttitude for Day #596: *Blessed are those who make the best of what they have on hand, for they shall be able to entertain themselves.*

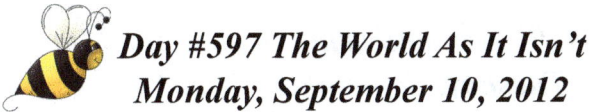

Day #597 The World As It Isn't
Monday, September 10, 2012

Someone sent me a link to one of those TED shows recently, and I thoroughly enjoyed "On Being Wrong," a speech by Kathryn Shultz in which she spoke about the value of recognizing that we make mistakes. One of the things she said, though, really struck home:

> "The miracle of your mind isn't that you can see the world as it is. It's that you can see the world as it isn't."

Her idea seemed to be (and I'll admit I may have missed something here) that this quality of being able to think into the future or the past, to use our imaginations, was what set human beings apart from other species. Maybe she didn't say exactly that, but I know there are folks out there who believe something along this line.

But then I read about Koko, the gorilla who knew sign language, talking in sign language about how she'd love to have a baby, or telling how she was sad when her good friend and fellow gorilla Michael died.

Or I read Jodi Picoult's beautiful, thought-provoking book *Lone Wolf*, and learn that wolves are capable of planning for the future.

The world as it is—and the world as it isn't—is a lot bigger than we think.

BeeAttitude for Day #597: *Blessed are those whose world is bigger than the inside of their head, for they shall live a rich, full life indeed.*

Day #598 Remembering September 11th
Tuesday, September 11, 2012

I firmly believe that if it's a person's time to leave this planet, nothing can hold that person back. I also believe that if it's NOT time for the soul to go on to other work, nothing and nobody can force a death to happen. That said, there still is no way to know when it's time.

On this day, besides remembering with deep respect the people (particularly the firefighters) who gave their lives, I like to think about all the people who missed the bus, didn't make the train, had a sick child and needed to stay home from work. People who missed their flight. People who quit their job the day before. All the people who would, should have been in those buildings, but who, for a higher reason that we do not and cannot understand, were not there.

I've experienced the death of a close friend only twice in my life. And I was with each of my parents when they died. Those four times were not events that affected you, however. Still, I know that, if you are of a certain age, you and I share a few deaths that hit everyone in this country and maybe even around the world. People older than I will recall exactly where they were when they learned that Pearl Harbor had been attacked. Maybe you do, or perhaps you'll remember only the last of these four dates:

- 11/22/1963 - I was a junior in high school, home sick for the first time that year. My mother called me from work and told me the president had been shot. I turned on the television and watched for the entire day, alternating between all three channels.

- 4/4/1968 - Living in Vermont. Unwilling to believe that MLK was gone.

- 6/6/1968 - RFK's assassination felt like a gut-kick. Twice in two months.

- 9/11/2001 - I was babysitting my 1-year-old granddaughter that day at my daughter's house.

Where were you for each of these events?

BeeAttitude for Day #598: *Blessed are those who do the job they're meant to do, and who love the work they do, for the honey they produce shall be sweet indeed.*

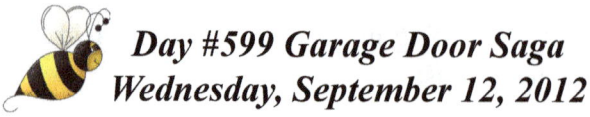

Day #599 Garage Door Saga
Wednesday, September 12, 2012

Pat Gerard, the archivist who is working on my papers (doesn't that sound official?), sent me a link last week when she read that I was being required by Gwinnett County to get rid of the "graffiti" on my garage doors. The link was to a site called the Mystery Fanfare blog.

This garage door library was painted in 2005 by artist Don Gray for the home of Lee Dembart (who was a former writer and book reviewer for the LA Times). I'd say it was completely appropriate.

I wish I had the courage (and the artistic talent) to do this, but I'm sure it would be labeled graffiti as well.

The tag line on Pat's email, by the way, was a quotation from Tennyson: Proverbs are "jewels five words long, that, on the stretched forefinger of time, sparkle forever."

I'd like to think that my BeeAttitudes will sparkle just as long.

My garage door went from looking like this:

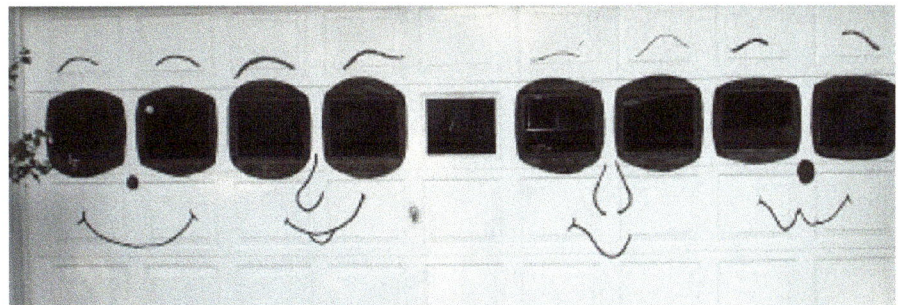

to looking like this:

to ending up like this (with the second coat of purple and the green around the windows):

Not a bad trade after all, I'd say. And now, I'm not going to say anything more about that door. Except to say that I painted the front door of my house purple, too!

BeeAttitude for Day #599: *Blessed are those who look on the bright side, the way we bees do, for they shall have sunny days despite the clouds.*

 ### *Day #600 Goodbye to the Bee Blog*
Thursday, September 13, 2012

Six hundred blog posts ago, I wasn't sure I'd get this far. Each evening, when I sat down to write the post for the next day, I simply cast around for whatever topic was on my mind, wrote about it, and scheduled it to publish the next morning at 12:01.

© Yelloideas Photography

Some entries were thoughtful, some informative; some were silly, others were sad. I never worried very much about what to say, though. After all, there was always going to be another day. Another day to be wiser. Another day to be better informed. Another day to shine. I'm a writer. I can always write. Right?

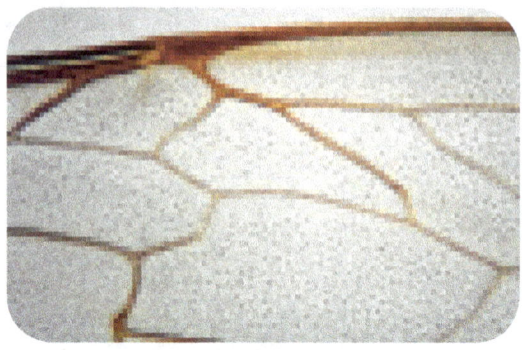

Well, all those other days have disappeared. I'm left with the knowledge that this will be my last post on this blog site, and I quite frankly don't know what to say.

I feel like I've already said it all. When you read this blog, you see me as I am. You know a great deal about my life—not just what's been happening for the past almost two years, but how my life has been shaped by the forces of history, of habit, of whimsy.

(Pexels.com)

I hope you've learned not only a great deal about bees, but a great deal about life itself, and I hope you realize, as I do, that there need never be an end to the learning.

(Pexels.com)

I leave you now, trusting that you'll keep in touch.

— If you've been with me from the beginning of the BeesKneesBeekeeping blog, I give you my deepest thanks.

— If you came in somewhere around the middle, I'm glad you joined the parade, and I encourage you to browse through the earlier posts.

— If you've been an occasional drop-in visitor to the blog, I do hope you've enjoyed your time(s) here.

— If you've left comments, I'd like you to know I've thoroughly enjoyed our conversations.

© Ofer Dahan (Pexels.com)

To borrow (and change) a line from an old song:

"The bees and I are whispering goodbye..."

BeeAttitude for Day #600: *Blessed are those who gather nectar when they say they will, for they shall collect rich yellow pollen along the way, and shall enrich the hive.*

Afterword

One lovely thing about a journey is that one never knows at the beginning just how far away the end point will be. Despite the fact that we schedule our vacations to last precisely this many days, or our business trips to begin on this day and end on that one, the journey we take may lead us far afield of what we expect before we take that first step.

That certainly was my experience as I looked at getting into beekeeping.

Throughout this journey, I've had support and encouragement from so many friends, and now, as I begin a new journey—that of founding my own publishing company—I feel equally encouraged. In 1869, Louisa May Alcott wrote, "I am no longer afraid of storms, for I have learned to sail my own ship."

Even now, My Own Ship Press is in its fledgling year, but the journey ahead of me will be a grand one, don't you think?

Thank you for having come along with me this far. Let's make the next day, the next week, the next year, the next decade, a resplendent adventure indeed.

Wishing you a fantastic journey,

>   --Fran
>   from my house beside a creek
>   on the other side of Hog Mountain

www.ingramcontent.com/pod-product-compliance
Lightning Source LLC
Chambersburg PA
CBHW051543020426
42333CB00016B/2071